THE HEART OF DAVID JOURNAL

Leading With Vision, Passion & Wisdom

VOLUME 4

By David Mayorga

Edited by Emily Rose King

Published by
SHABAR PUBLICATIONS
www.shabarpublications.com

CONTENTS

Volume 4

1

Dust of the Ground!

And the Lord God formed man of the dust of the ground and breathed into his nostrils the breath of life; and man became a living being." (Genesis 2:7)

After walking with the Lord for some time, I have come to realize one of the most powerful secrets to a life of power and blessing.

In God's kingdom, everything is upside down.

Some call it the "Upside-Down Kingdom." For example: If you desire to be first, you must be last; if one desires to lead, they must first be the servant of all; and if you want to have more, one must give more! Do you get me? These paradoxes are found in principle, all over the Bible.

One day, while meditating on the Scripture above, something came to me, something I want to share with you.

The Lord began to unfold this truth to me, and this is what He said, "David, unless you understand your original place of origin, you will not understand your purpose and destiny for what I want to do IN you and through you."

At first, I was puzzled.

Then I realized that to be filled with the wind [breath] of God, one must realize where they came from and what they were made of. In the case of Adam, the first man created, God made him out of dust.

There is really nothing pretty to look at in a clump of dust or dirt. Surely, this does not make any kind of impression! At least not to the natural world.

Now in the mind of God or God's design, this was a must!

Man had to be made out of nothing so that God could be everything!

Man had to realize that He was made by the hand of God, and he was not man making or creating himself. This is a valuable lesson, if one is to ever walk in God's power.

God's power is resident in everyone who is born-again, or perhaps I should say, the potential to be powerful in God, is within us who believe.

To the degree that one realizes his state as dust, is to the degree that His breath can literally blow through us.

I have seen through the years how believers tend to rise or make the effort to rise above their God-given sphere or calling.

They swear that God told them to do this or do that, but in the end, it all comes out! It was nothing more than self, greed, and selfish ambition!

Recognizing our origin as dust, is such a valuable revelation, and let me tell you why.

When one realizes that he or she is nothing but dust, and had it not been for the breath of God blowing in us and through us, we would all be worthless!

The realization of knowing where we came from – is such a key component to our destiny in God.

Neh'enah.

2

Deep Subtle Rest!

"Then the Lord God took the man and put him in the garden of Eden to tend and keep it." (Genesis 2:15)

During my quiet time with God, my spirit was awakened to one of the many realities of how God leads His servants into His plan and purpose.

In following God's will, one will always know he or she is in the right place with God because of the overwhelming inner peace one feels.

To not have peace in your heart after taking a decision or making a choice, is to know that God has gone one way and you have gone another!

Obviously, our goal is to please God in all the things He

is asking us to do. Our goal is to walk and live in God's favor always.

God Took Man . . .

In my encounter with God's words, I discovered that God had instituted a great plan for mankind.

Before he turned man loose to their purpose, He first created a garden, a garden called the garden of Eden.

After God created a garden, He then created man and placed him inside that garden. Man's first calling was to tend and keep the garden of Eden.

From God's perspective, this is a great plan and satisfying to the heart of God. Isn't this why man was created? To bring joy to the heart of God. Of course, it is!

God Put Man In . . .

I know that people often ask the question, "What is God's

will for my life?" Or, "I wonder what God wants me to do for Him?" These questions usually tend to leave believers wondering and guessing about God's plan for their lives. As we read the text above, we will discover two things:

The first thing is this, "God took man."

What this means is that God knew exactly what He would do with His creation; God would be taking man and/or handpicking him for a clear purpose – to tend and keep the garden.

The second thing we learn from this passage is that God Himself put Man in the garden of Eden. This wasn't by mistake, but rather by divine design.

Now the word, "put," in the original Hebrew, means – to rest.

The Call to Rest

If you have not understood the message yet, let me shed

some light onto it.

When God calls a man or a woman for some kind of service, what God is really saying is, "I'm going to use you —so let me take you to another place (level) and put you in that place. This will be a place of rest. It will never be a place of turmoil."

If God is moving you and placing you, then the place doesn't matter for you, and you will always know it's God by the deep subtle rest you will receive from obeying God. Meditate on this.

Neh'enah.

3

Back to the Altar!

"But the Lord plagued Pharaoh and his house with great plagues because of Sarai, Abram's wife. And Pharaoh called Abram and said, 'What is this you have done to me? Why did you not tell me that she was your wife? Why did you say, 'She is my sister'? I might have taken her as my wife. Now therefore, here is your wife; take her and go your way." So Pharaoh commanded his men concerning him, and they sent him away, with his wife and all that he had. Then Abram went up from Egypt, he and his wife, and all that he had, and Lot with him, to the South. Abram was very rich in livestock, in silver, and in gold. And he went on his journey from the South as far as Bethel, to the place where his tent had been at the beginning, between Bethel and Ai, to the place of the altar which he had made there at first. And there Abram called on the name of the Lord." (Genesis 12:17-13:4)

Contemplating upon the rich life of Abram this morning in my quiet time, I came to realize one incredible point.

After Abram had made his way to Egypt, he was confronted by the Pharaoh. Abram was afraid that they might take Sarai—so he lied to the Pharaoh. He told the Pharaoh that Sarai was his sister and not his wife.

I don't really know what the Pharaoh was thinking of doing to Sarai, but God did not permit any wrongdoing to be done to Sarai.

As a matter of fact, the Scripture says that God plagued Pharaoh and his house with great plagues because of Sarai.

Finally, Pharaoh figured it out and called Abram and confronted him, "What is this you have done to me? Why did you not tell me that she was your wife? Why did you say, 'She is my sister'? I might have taken her as my wife."

As a result of this one confrontation, Pharaoh released

Abram and everything that belonged to him. Abram recognized that he had gotten himself into some serious trouble and ended up lying to Pharaoh and almost made a disgrace out of this trip to Egypt.

What Did Abram Learn?

Well, another lesson is laid out for us:

Abram went from Egypt and came back from the South between Bethel and Ai, back to the tent that he had made from the beginning. Yes, he came back to the place where the altar he had first made, and there he called upon the Lord.

There is nothing more awesome than for one to find the place where he can restore his broken and shattered heart.

There is no other place in the world that can enrich the human heart but at the altar of sacrifice in the presence of a holy God.

Abram found God one more time and I'm sure he repented and fell prostrate before Almighty God!

Run Back to God!

Abram knew he had faltered; he knew he had crossed the line and had it not been for God's mercy and ever-lasting compassion, he would have been dead.

We can learn that even though we miss God, the Lord Himself will not allow our destiny to go sour.

Though we live in stupor and selfishness, God will see the heart and the shame and the powerlessness in us to make the significant change – and He will step in with unmerited mercy and make a way for us, where there is no way!

The Scripture says that God will not despise a contrite and broken spirit. Aren't you glad for his ever-increasing, ever-expanding love? Run back to Him! Neh'enah.

Volume 4

4

For All the Land Which You See, I Will Give to You!

"So Abram said to Lot, 'Please let there be no strife between you and me, and between my herdsmen and your herdsmen; for we are brethren. Is not the whole land before you? Please separate from me. If you take the left, then I will go to the right; or, if you go to the right, then I will go to the left.'" (Genesis 13:8-9)

When one walks in the favor of the Lord, one's attitude towards life is very different from the person who is not walking in His favor.

Walking in God's favor and knowing it, makes all the difference when it comes to your destiny in God.

Let me share with you what I believe God is calling all of

His servants to embrace. To start, embracing God's favor and fully trusting God in your relationship with Him is key to understanding what God wants to accomplish in you.

In the story mentioned above, God had this awesome relationship with Abram.

Abram has been learning what it means to trust God with his life and with his future. This is not an easy thing to do, unless you truly see God as He is!

I believe Abram had received such revelation, and that is why he could enter into all that God had designed for him.

The challenge and proof that Abram had arrived to a higher dimension in God is this: The land got too crowded for Abram and Lot.

Their herdsmen were at odds and were fighting over territory. It was time for them to separate, but God didn't have a meeting with both of them. God only met with Abram. Why only with Abram? Because Abram was the man with the revelatory knowledge of who God is!

The Lord will always speak to us when we have reached the level of understanding His heart.

Abram knew that he belonged to God and that he could trust God with everything.

In the separation between Abram and his nephew Lot, Abram gave Lot the first choice: In essence, Abram told Lot, "Choose whatever piece of territory you want. Whatever side you choose, I will choose the opposite side."

Do you see this? Abram was not worried about taking any particular side. He understood that his own life was not dependent upon sides and that his success was not contingent upon what the eye could see and reason. Abram trusted God fully!

As soon as Lot made his choice, God spoke to Abram. God never left Abram to wonder what was going to happen with his future, no sir! Immediately God spoke and released one of the most powerful promises given to man.

Listen to this: **"And the Lord said to Abram, after Lot had separated from him: 'Lift your eyes now and look from the place where you are—northward, southward, eastward, and westward; for all the land which you see I give to you and your descendants forever. And I will make your descendants as the dust of the earth; so that if a man could number the dust of the earth, then your descendants also could be numbered. Arise, walk in the land through its length and its width, for I give it to you.'"** (Genesis 13:14-17)

When the time comes to separate from anything —try to remember this story. If we trust God with our lives, then we can follow His lead. The point is this: God will always take care of those who take care of their relationship with Him! Neh'enah.

5

I Go Childless...!

"After these things the word of the Lord came to Abram in a vision, saying, 'Do not be afraid, Abram. I am your shield, your exceedingly great reward.' But Abram said, 'Lord God, what will You give me, seeing I go childless, and the heir of my house is Eliezer of Damascus?' Then Abram said, 'Look, You have given me no offspring; indeed one born in my house is my heir!' And behold, the word of the Lord came to him, saying, 'This one shall not be your heir, but one who will come from your own body shall be your heir.' Then He brought him outside and said, 'Look now toward heaven, and count the stars if you are able to number them.' And He said to him, 'So shall your descendants be.' And he believed in the Lord, and He accounted it to him for righteousness." (Genesis 15:1-6)

Nothing pressures people more than the feeling that their lives are being wasted and nothing has been accomplished up to date! Have you ever felt this sinking feeling? I believe that most of us have walked in these shoes.

The feeling of worthlessness coupled with the inability to make anything happen can be devastating to anyone, especially to an individual who has received prophetic promises and the like.

The God Factor

In walking with the Lord, one must continually walk in humility before God.

The expectations for any promise of God, should always be high. Yet, too often, those promises are delayed.

It is here where the sinking feeling of despair enters with such force, that it makes one really doubt and wonder what the hold-up is!

When the promise is made by God, whether it be through dreams, prophetic words, or a personal promise from the Holy Spirit, one must embrace it and cultivate it the best way they can.

Sometimes praying back the promise, will cultivate it and keep it near your heart. I have seen this help me in my own walk of faith.

If God has promised you something, you can bank on it! God is not into playing games with anyone on matters that affect our destiny, our future, and/or eternity.

Abraham's Test and God's Delay

Though Abraham had a visitation from the Lord during the waiting time for the promise to come, he still had many questions. The question of time, the question of how all this would eventually come to pass, etc.

All these questions are legit when one is trying to find

their way through God's will. How will the promise be fulfilled?!

We really don't know why God does things in certain ways, but all we can say is that God is faithful and will bring forth His promise in due season. It almost seems that God desires that we stay close to Him through the process.

His delays have always confounded the believer, and His timing carries even a greater mystery.

Yet, in spite of all that we feel and see with our natural faculties, His divine order continues to outlast our human strength and our ability to comprehend.

My dear friends, there is no mistaking the message to those who have set their hearts on following Jesus – it is all about intimacy.

It's never been about the promise, nor when it will be fulfilled. It's about knowing God in a deeper way! Neh'enah.

6

Are You Still in the Faith?

"Therefore do not worry, saying, 'What shall we eat?' or 'What shall we drink?' or 'What shall we wear?' For after all these things the Gentiles seek. For your heavenly Father knows that you need all these things. But seek first the kingdom of God and His righteousness, and all these things shall be added to you." (Matthew 6:31-33)

God's people should not be concerned about earthly matters as much as they should be concerned with heavenly matters.

You see, everything starts in the spiritual realm. Nothing that was created came from an earthly idea; it all came from the spiritual realm.

When Jesus begins to bring forth this revelation of not worrying, He begins to compare two ideas —the earthly and the heavenly.

He first makes His point to the believer who tends to lower his realm and wonders about all the natural things. It is easy to lower yourself to the earthly.

One of the reasons that prayer is stressed in the local gatherings is because it keeps us in the realm of the spirit.

Here are some things that carnality longs and cries for:

1. What Shall We Eat? What shall we drink?

For the natural mind, food and drink intake seem to always be at the top of the list. We are usually overly concerned about what we are going to eat and drink and how much of it.

When we are being carnally-minded, this always seems to be the concern. Food and drink have a very funny way of tranquilizing our anxieties and worries.

I can surely understand why the Gentiles were concerned over their supply of food and drink.

When one walks in the kingdom of God and fully understands that their King will provide them food and drink, these particular worries dissipate.

2. What Shall we wear?

Outward appearance seems to also be a thing to worry about if you are a Gentile.

Too many times we worry about what other people see but have very little concern with what God sees when He looks inside our hearts.

It is amazing what the carnal mind conceives within us!

When one comes into the kingdom of God, one takes a new position; it's the position of royalty. One never needs to worry about performing for anyone, putting up a front or façade.

We can hide behind Christ the King and say, "In Him we live and move and have our being."

Here's what we must come to grips with…

Gentiles seek the natural things of life, for their vision is earthly. They have passions and desires, but they are for the most part, fleshly in nature.

The Gentiles are unable to rise above the earthly, for they are yet to know the kingdom of God, for they have not been born-again of the Spirit of God.

The born-again believer has caught a glimpse of eternity and thus lives according to that standard.

If you are born-again and find yourself lusting after earthly things, it would be a wise thing to evaluate and see if you are still in the faith, or for a lack of better terms, if you are still walking in the level of faith where God's people should be dwelling.

Neh'enah.

7

It Might Take All Night!

"Then Jacob was left alone; and a Man wrestled with him until the breaking of day." (Genesis 32:24)

For some reason, reading about Jacob's life, I always get the sense that this man spent the second part of his life learning (in a deeper way) about himself, about God, and his ultimate call and purpose in life.

Apparently, as a young man, Jacob was not a very nice person. His name alone said it all! He was a deceiver. He stole his brother's birthright and his brother's first-born's blessing. He was selfish and all he thought of —was of himself.

In dealing with self, it would probably be safe to say that all of us have been at the same place Jacob was at one time or another. We have all drank and tasted from the awful, well of egocentricity.

After walking in selfishness for quite some time, Jacob finally gets himself in a heap of trouble.

His brother Esau hates him and wants to kill him. Jacob had now crossed the line; he ended up running away from his brother Esau who was ready to kill him, due to his selfishness of course.

Selfishness has the potential to affect us in so many negative ways. If we allow ourselves to be directed by it – it will pay us badly!

Self Doesn't Know When to Stop!

All of us have been born with sinful nature. This nature is filled with us (self) in mind. We think of us first, we do for us first, it's all about us; it cries, "Me, me, me!"

The flesh or self is like a fire, it doesn't know when to stop. Its hunger is never ending; the appetite of self is like a consuming fire.

> **"There are three things that are never satisfied,**
> **Four never say, 'Enough!':**
> **The grave,**
> **The barren womb,**
> **The earth that is not satisfied with water—**
> **And the fire never says, "Enough!"** (Proverbs 30:15-16)

In the life of Jacob, from what we know as we read, is that Jacob's life was enslaved by self.

The man was all about himself until we reached Genesis 32:24.

It was at this particular place in Jacob's life that he was finally confronted by the Lord.

The Fight of a Lifetime!

"... and a Man wrestled with him until the breaking of day." (Genesis 32:24b)

I believe that there was nothing that could have prepared Jacob for this great fight with God Himself. When Jacob least expected it, God met Him!

The Man who wrestled with Jacob was the very Son of God!

This formulates the picture of the old man being broken, allowing for the new man to come in and reign in him.

As you can read, it wasn't a ten-minute brawl, no sir, they fought till the breaking of day!

The quicker one recognizes his own true condition, the quicker the breaking and restoration take place. The longer it takes us to see our real self, the longer it takes for our destiny to align with God's plans.

He Will Always Get You Alone!

One of the things I have come to appreciate in God is this – to spend time alone in His presence. This is the place where all breaking will take place, and all restoration will be consummated!

To be alone with God is not an easy challenge for God's servant.

God will search you out and deal with anything that is not of His nature! He will purge us first, but then He will heal us, that we may stand by His power and in His power alone!

Neh'enah.

8

The Dream Killers! Part 1

"Now when they saw him [Joseph] afar off, even before he came near them, they conspired against him to kill him. Then they said to one another, 'Look, this dreamer is coming! Come therefore, let us now kill him and cast him into some pit; and we shall say, "Some wild beast has devoured him."

We shall see what will become of his dreams!'" (Genesis 37:18-20)

Pondering the life of Joseph in Genesis 37, my eyes were opened once more, and my heart broken by the countless obstacles arrayed against every dreamer who has walked with God in years passed.

As I continued to study this chapter, I quickly saw the pattern and learned how the devil has used many things to bring God-given dreams to an end.

Whether it might be an inward battle or an external attack against a dreamer, it is intentional and its end result is to destroy the kingdom's advancement upon the earth.

We must understand that the enemy's vision is intentional and filled with fury and hatred toward everything that God has initiated.

If you are presently pregnant with God's dream— you must be intentional in bringing this dream to pass. You must fight to defend your spiritual womb!

Remember, the devil wants you to abort what you are carrying inside!

Joseph was highly favored by his father Jacob. He had been given a tunic of many colors, and I'm thinking to myself that there was probably not another one like it!

This young man had been touched by God, and his father attested to this by granting him favor.

Obviously, his eleven brothers were not too happy over this. As a matter of fact, they hated him and wanted to dispose of him.

Nothing triggers jealousy and envy in our hearts more than when we see others being blessed and used by God in ministry, business, or entering into great opportunities.

Please notice the Scripture mentioned above: **"Come therefore, let us now kill him and cast him into some pit; and we shall say, 'Some wild beast has devoured him.' We shall see what will become of his dreams!"**

I read this portion before I started writing this devotion, and it made my heart break. The words, **"We shall see what will become of his dreams!"** brought memories of my early childhood.

Abandoned by my mother and raised by my grandparents, I had every reason to excuse myself and die of despair, loneliness, and rejection.

Yet through God's grace alone, and prophetic destiny for my life, He raised me up in the midst of a broken situation.

Always know that you were born for a purpose in God.

When God created you, it was intentional. You will discover His plan and purpose as you seek His face and become more attentive to the voice of the Holy Spirit.

Don't let anything or anyone kill your God-given dreams – nothing!

Neh'enah.

9

The Dream Killers! Part 2

"We shall see what will become of his dreams." (Genesis 37:20)

I have been walking with God for a good while now, and I have come to the place in my own walk with God to know that every God-given vision will be tested.

God will allow every dream to be put through fire, and those who care to fight for their God-given dream will see the good of the land.

If you are walking in God's divine order, you will be a recipient of many revelations and visions of the Lord. God will speak prophetic dreams to you time and time again.

The servant of God must know that one needs to be positioned to see them come to pass.

I have also noticed that in my endeavor to see God's dream come to pass, I have to overcome some of the most vicious tactics the enemy, my flesh, and the world have arrayed against me.

Let me share with you a few that I have personally encountered…

Methods of killing God-given dreams:

Criticism from Friends. **"And one shall say unto him, 'What are these wounds in thine hands? Then he shall answer, 'Those with which I was wounded in the house of my friends."** (Zechariah 13:6)

Coming under attack and severe criticism from friends has to be one of the most challenging things to overcome as a servant of the Lord.

I have seen this in my own life and how people who call

themselves "friends" have spoken curses and have disrespected me and my family.

People who I have entrusted with my ministry and life have arrayed against everything I have stood for.

This can be very heartbreaking, and if it had not been for the grace of God – my whole vision of serving Jesus would have ceased.

Envy from People Around You. **"A tranquil heart gives life to the flesh, but envy makes the bones rot."** (Proverbs 14:30)

The dictionary describes envy as a feeling of discontented or resentful longing aroused by someone else's possessions, qualities, or luck.
Envy has to be one of the most wicked forces that makes other people come against you.

Just because they couldn't get it done! - they don't want you to succeed.

Envy happens to people when they had the opportunity initially, but then squandered it; then you came along and made it happen! This breeds envy in the fleshly heart!

If you let an envious individual get under your skin, you might end up aborting your own dream or vision.

Fear & Doubt Instilled by Satan. **"But when he saw the strength of the wind, he was afraid, and beginning to sink he cried out, 'Lord, save me!'"** (Matthew 14:30)

There will always be always fear – the great paralyzer!

Satan uses the tool of fear to paralyze anything that is holy and divine. He is always and forever instilling doubt and fear on God's servants.

Satan's desire is to make God's servant doubt that God is able to take them through.

Once God's child takes his eyes off Jesus, he will begin to sink into discouragement. He will fall into despair and along with him, God's given dream!

Majoring on Minors. **"Woe unto you, scribes and Pharisees, hypocrites! For ye pay tithe of mint and anise and cummin, and have omitted the weightier matters of the law, judgment, mercy, and faith: these ought ye to have done, and not to leave the other undone. Ye blind guides, which strain at a gnat, and swallow a camel."** (Matthew 23:23-24)

One of the things that I have seen in my own life is this thing about being busy with things God never told me to do.

We leave the important to attend to the urgent, and then we come back to the important, still hoping things have remained the same... and they don't stay the same.

We lose ground when we go after the lesser things.

We must keep God's dream ahead of us and attend to it on a daily basis. We cannot afford to lose focus on what God has promised us.

Unworthiness. **"...and giving joyful thanks to the Father, who has qualified you to share in the inheritance of his holy people in the kingdom of light."** (Colossians 1:12)

Nothing hangs over someone's head like the feeling of worthlessness . Worthless to friends, worthless to family and friends and yes, worthless to God.
Many visions have died in this pit!

I truly believe that this deep emotion is embedded in our minds because of our lack of faith in the finished work of Christ.

When Jesus died for us, He paid the full price for our forgiveness of our sins.

Along with that, Jesus also made provision for us to be justified and with this, return the Father's house and live in it forever! Access has been granted for us! Hallelujah.

Remember this the next time the devil comes around making you feel unworthy, - instead, tell him, "I am worthy because of what Jesus has done, it's not because of me!"

So stand in the finished work of Christ!

Neh'enah.

10

The Dream Killers! Part 3

"We shall see what will become of his dreams. So it came to pass, when Joseph had come to his brothers, that they stripped Joseph of his tunic, the tunic of many colors that was on him. Then they took him and cast him into a pit. And the pit was empty; there was no water in it." (Genesis 37:20, 23, 24)

In my last meditation, I covered how Joseph was highly favored by his father. As a result of the favor upon his life, his eleven brothers were not too happy with him.

It was at this time that the brothers wanted to dispose of their young brother and remove him for good.

They thought about killing him, and they would have killed him except for one of their brothers (Reuben) who stepped in and stopped them. Listen to this: **"But Reuben heard it, and he delivered him out of their hands, and said, 'Let us not kill him.'**

And Reuben said to them, 'Shed no blood, but cast him into this pit which is in the wilderness, and do not lay a hand on him—that he might deliver him out of their hands, and bring him back to his father.'" (Genesis 37:21, 22)

One of the things that I have seen in Scripture and in my own life is this: God always makes a way for his favored ones.

He will always send someone to open an unknown door, change the weather patterns, anything to keep his servant flowing in the right direction.

If you will take notice, the Lord always goes before His called-out ones. He is constantly surrounding them with people, situations, or events that bring them out and into

His perfect will.
You might be going through a very hard situation today, and you might be facing the greatest battle against sin you have ever faced.

You might be emotionally dry or spiritually empty – you would rather just quit on everything you are called to do and run to the hills and hide from the tempest and the storm; it might feel like your own tunic of many colors has been stripped by the adversity, by those who have had ill-will intentions towards you —let me tell you something— though you are presently in a pit today, remember two things:

1. The pit has no water in it - you are not going to drown. (Genesis 37:24)

2. Know that there is a "Rueben" in your life whose sole intent is to look after you and rescue you. If he is not there with you today, he is on his way! (Genesis 37:21, 22)

Be encouraged, my friend. The Lord will not let you slip. He is not finished with you yet. Your dream will come to pass!

Neh'enah.

11

That Is All I Have Jesus!

"Now Jesus called His disciples to Himself and said, 'I have compassion on the multitude, because they have now continued with Me three days and have nothing to eat. And I do not want to send them away hungry, lest they faint on the way.' Then His disciples said to Him, 'Where could we get enough bread in the wilderness to fill such a great multitude?' Jesus said to them, 'How many loaves do you have?' And they said, 'Seven, and a few little fish.' (Matthew 15:32-34)

When it comes to the call of God on an individual's life, we have to go back to God's original intent for creating every man and woman.

God has given everything He created a special assignment.

We have all been made to serve our heavenly Father with who we are. It is here that we must understand when God made us in His image, He also made us in such a way, that we would be able to express Himself through our talents and abilities.

Many have said through the years, "I am not able; I am not worthy; I am not equipped; I am not a student of Your Word," and the list goes on and on regarding all the excuses we human beings come up with when it comes to serving God.

Obedience that Transcends

While believers make the attempt to figure out what is what they are supposed to do for God – there are others simply hearing and obeying God!

Simple faith and simple obedience are truly the highway for God's will to be carried out here on earth.

For example, let us take the story that I am using as text

for this devotion.

His disciples were hard working men (they were tax-collectors, fishermen, etc.) before they became disciples of Jesus. No one was in the ministry before Jesus manifested Himself at the Jordan River.

Be the Vessel God Needs for the Hour!

Yet when the need arose in the heart of God to feed the multitudes, He didn't call the cafeteria manager or Israel's finest chefs; He called His disciples, yes, these untrained men who were nobodies, according to worldly standards.

Were they prepared for such an hour? The obvious answer is – No! They were not. Yet Jesus only needed their willingness and what they had at hand!

How Many Loaves Do You Have?

Jesus never looked at the external need. If He was to dare

and do this, He would probably have gotten very discouraged!

He didn't take a head count before feeding the multitudes; He took a heart count and wondered how much faith His disciples had, and if they were willing to step out into the unknown!

We must never let the external (circumstances, adversities) dictate what God can do or put to test the abundance of God. God doesn't give according to need, but according to our revelation of who He is!

If "seven [loaves] and a few little fish," is all we have, then that is all He needs from us!

Neh'enah.

12

Intentional Intimacy!

"For You do not desire sacrifice, or else I would give it;
You do not delight in burnt offering.
The sacrifices of God are a broken spirit,
A broken and a contrite heart—
These, O God, You will not despise." (Psalm 51:16-17)

In this particular meditation or devotion, you will find King David's prayer after he had confessed to his adultery and the murder of Bathsheba's husband.

David had had many low points in his life and in this particular low point, as he had failed in his morals, it's obvious that this man is totally devastated!

Here's what I discovered as I pursued the heart of God in this matter: Is David really concerned about what people will think of his failure? Is David really worried about what this would do to his kingship?

I dare to believe that David didn't care about any of that. I might be wrong, but seeing David's trajectory with God, I venture to say that David was only concerned about what God thought of him.

David knew what God was looking for. He understood that God wasn't impressed with any one thing that man could create or offer Him. Yes, David had been so intimate with God that he didn't need to be reminded of God's expectations.

So what is this one thing that God is looking for in all His servants? What is the door to a life of joy in the Lord? A brightened countenance? A life of power and purpose?

In my pursuit of God, I have come to know that all these things can be attained and maintained by nothing more and nothing less, than a life of intimate prayer and devotion to Jesus.

Whether a servant of God fails in their morals, in their standards, in their devotion, in their task, or in any endeavor in life – intentional intimacy, will always open the doors of heaven!

Shabar!

The Scripture says that, **"... a broken spirit; a broken and contrite heart- These, Oh God, You will not despise."**

The word for broken in Hebrew is the word Shabar which means to break, break into pieces.

I believe that unless God's servant realizes their real position before God, the servant will always run the risk of thinking that He has no need for continual intimacy with God.

The servant of God must live a life that is continually broken before God, so that He may avail Himself of the nature and power of God in his life.

Unless the servant is willing to be broken by God on a daily basis, the servant will always run the risk of living for their own desires.

I know this may sound extreme, but trust me, the flesh cannot be trusted.

Daily intimacy with God keeps the flesh in check! Prayer must be the kind of prayer that breaks you of all fleshly desire, ambition, and selfishness.

A broken life is a life that has allowed God to come and take full charge of that servant's dreams, ambitions, plans, goals, endeavors, everything that man can ever imagine in his finite mind!

Once under the pressure of the process, one must not whine, complain, or cry about its violent pain! Just drink your cup of pain in silence, and you will be rewarded openly! "Blessed is the man who can drink his cup without blaming others for it!"

As I close these thoughts, I am reminded of Leonard Ravenhill's writings where he once wrote: "When a man stops praying, he starts sinning. When a man starts praying, He will stop sinning." So true!

Neh'enah.

13

Eyes on Eternity!

"From that time Jesus began to show to His disciples that He must go to Jerusalem, and suffer many things from the elders and chief priests and scribes, and be killed, and be raised the third day. Then Peter took Him aside and began to rebuke Him, saying, 'Far be it from You, Lord; this shall not happen to You!' But He turned and said to Peter, 'Get behind Me, Satan! You are an offense to Me, for you are not mindful of the things of God, but the things of men.'" (Matthew 16:21-23)

Here are some interesting thoughts: While all the people outside of Christ saw the natural order of things, Christ saw the spiritual distinctives. The worldview that Jesus had was not of this world.

His whole being had been raised in power of the Holy

Spirit to the effect that every faculty in His body was tuned to what mattered most—this would be eternity. His eyes and ears, His heart and mind, His feet and hands, they were all geared with a rare fuel — the fuel of eternity!

To understand Christ's mission and to fully appreciate God's intent, one must first understand His view on eternity. Moreover, in the same sense, for one to grasp eternity and what is of eternal value, one must understand and watch Christ's actions here on earth.

Everything He did was intentional; everything was fueled by the eternity in His heart.

As Jesus begins to speak to His disciples regarding the upcoming adversities and trials that awaited Him, Peter doesn't get it.

Peter saw things from an earthly perspective. Peter, in essence, is saying "Jesus, you are my friend, my buddy! No one is going to hurt you. You are a good guy and you don't deserve this harsh treatment you are speaking of. I will defend you to the end!"

I believe Peter meant well. I believe Peter didn't mean any harm by his words. The only thing is that Peter's mindset was not God's mindset.

Herein lies the problem with many so-called followers of Jesus!

The Lord is speaking a language saturated with eternal values —while the "Spirit-less believer" is thinking about how to preserve and make the most of his life here on earth. (Not to be confused with kingdom advancement [which is world evangelization] as it is written in Matthew 28:18-20, where Jesus commands us to go!)

Occupied with the Things of God

The truly Spirit-filled life has a few things in view – to please God by hearing His voice and doing His bidding on earth.

Jesus is saying to the disciples, "I'm about to be arrested and killed; but I will rise again after the third day. It is necessary for this to happen so that access can be granted for all who believe and regain the benefits which were lost in the Garden of Eden!"

Jesus' mindset was occupied with the restoration process of all humanity; Peter was occupied with making sure he didn't lose his friend and mentor.

We are forever trying to protect ourselves from possible losses; yet God continues to remind us to not worry about a thing!

Occupied with the Things of Men

Finally, Jesus has to put Peter in his place, and tells him, **"Get behind Me, Satan! You are an offense to Me, for you are not mindful of the things of God, but the things of men."**

Not that Peter was possessed by the devil, but he was being influenced mightily by a fleshly, carnal mindset. Jesus said to Peter, you are an offense to Me! The word offense (GR.) means "cause of ruin."

Jesus was calling Peter out and really saying, "Your carnal mind, your fleshly mindset, will be the "cause of ruin" for all that our heavenly Father has planned out for all humanity!"

In closing, we must always make the effort, or at least push through, to get to the secret place of prayer; that place where we can come in and shut the door and hear the Father's heart.

I believe our destiny is wrapped-up in being intimate with God.

Neh'enah.

14

No Strings Attached!

"So Pharaoh said, 'I will let you go, that you may sacrifice to the Lord your God in the wilderness; only you shall not go very far away. Intercede for me.'" (Exodus 8:28)

In pondering the enslavement of God's people and how Pharaoh had them under hard work and bondage, nothing changes my mind that Egypt is definitely the symbol of slavery.

All through the Word of God we find Egypt as a type and shadow of the world, the flesh and everything that is anti-Christ.

It was out of Egypt that God brought His children and spiritually speaking, it is the same with us, He brought us out of a world of sin and selfishness, and transferred us into a kingdom of light.

In my meditation today, I caught a glimpse of something; let me share it with you:

When Moses starts to take leadership on behalf of God's people as their "deliverer," he makes a request to Pharaoh – the request was to release God's children so they could serve Him, **"The Lord God of the Hebrews has sent me to you, saying, 'Let My people go, that they may serve Me in the wilderness...'"** (Exodus 7:16)

To this Pharaoh would not agree, thus the plagues were unleashed upon him and Egypt.

Finally, Pharaoh consents but with strings attached. Pharaoh is willing to allow Moses and God's children to go and have a time of sacrifice and worship in the wilderness, but adds, **"only you shall not go very far away."**

What does this mean for you and I?

For starters here are some words in Hebrew that will help us define the real intent of Pharaoh - the words **"not very far away"** means rachaq a prim. root; to be or become far or distant: —abandon.

Can you imagine the Pharaoh telling Moses, Don't go worship! You will become what you worship! If you become what you worship, that means you will be far away from me; then you will abandon me!

I'm challenging your heart today! Find a secret place where you can seek the face of God, yes, a place far away from the natural, earthly, and cold world!

No matter what your flesh is crying out for, go far away and meet God! It's time to rise above your fears, doubts, and disbelief!

My dear friend, if you haven't gotten a hold of this yet, it's time to get it: the devil hates the fact that you go far away [into your secret place of intimacy to meet God] —The devil feels abandoned every single time you draw near to the Father!

Neh'enah.

15

What Am I Still Missing?

"Now behold, one came and said to Him, 'Good Teacher, what good thing shall I do that I may have eternal life?'

So He said to him, 'Why do you call Me good? No one is good but One, that is, God. But if you want to enter into life, keep the commandments.'

He said to Him, 'Which ones?'

Jesus said, 'You shall not murder:You shall not commit adultery:You shall not steal,:You shall not bear false witness: Honor your father and your mother: and You shall love your neighbor as yourself.'

The young man said to Him, 'All these things I have kept from my youth. What do I still lack?'

Jesus said to him, 'If you want to be perfect, go, sell what you have and give to the poor, and you will have treasure in heaven; and come, follow Me.'

But when the young man heard that saying, he went away sorrowful, for he had great possessions." (Matthew 19:16-22)

In my meditation today, I came across a very interesting portion of Scripture, one that I have often read and pondered deeply.

Though I had visited this story before, today was a bit different. I had the sense that God was reaching out to me and bringing forth some insight.

What Do I Still Lack?

Through reading this story one can infer that this individual, who seemed to be rich, was looking for something else, something more significant.

Apparently, the riches he possessed were not enough to fill his empty soul, so he searched for something more.

This same young man comes to Jesus and asks the Lord, "What good thing shall I do that I may have eternal life?"

It is life that he is looking for; his soul is longing for true substance!

You see, we can all convince ourselves that we have gained much by trying hard. We can all say that we got a great deal out of life!

Yet, in all our findings, we will also discover that not everything that we have gained is of eternal value or life-giving power!

Things give us a short-lived temporal emotion of success and achievement, yet with no power to sustain us over the long-haul.

This young man had rejoiced over his accomplishment, but only for a moment.

Finally, it was time to face the facts: He had no life or anything of eternal value, that he could make claims for.

Many believers today are in the same predicament.

They boast of great accomplishments, but the Lord never gave them that! The Lord was never involved in the pursuit of selfish goals and ambitions. It was all initiated by a carnal desire without the present Spirit of God.

Still Thirsty or Hungry?

Unless the Lord is the One filling your soul with His manna, then you will never have true nourishment for your soul.

Unless the Lord is the One depositing heavenly vision into your heart, all you will have is great fleshly ideas which

will only lead you to move in spectacular fleshly ways and receive applause from fleshly people!
The young man said that he had kept the commandments from his youth, yet he was still empty and lifeless! He received fresh commandments from God, but why was he still life-less?

I believe He was life-less because He never walked out the revelation that God had given him.

Life-less!

Here is what I have learned in my walk: Unless we are obedient to the present-day revelation that God is giving to us, we will continue to remain lifeless.

We will always lack, even if we have heard the word one-million times. Life begins when we start walking it out!

Walking by Revelation

Eating God's words means that we are literally walking out what God is telling us to do. Obedience to the Father's heart is eating heavenly food.

When we live this way, we don't go around hungry or thirsty! We don't go around looking for sympathy and love and acceptance when we are walking in God's revelation.

We can all hear and learn God's Word— but it's not until we walk it out, that the Father's will in us is manifested. This alone will produce life in us!

Neh'enah.

16

It's More Than an Emotion!

"Now all the people witnessed the thunderings, the lightning flashes, the sound of the trumpet, and the mountain smoking; and when the people saw it, they trembled and stood afar off. Then they said to Moses, 'You speak with us, and we will hear; but let not God speak with us, lest we die.' And Moses said to the people, 'Do not fear; for God has come to test you, and that His fear may be before you, so that you may not sin.' So the people stood afar off, but Moses drew near the thick darkness where God was." (Exodus 20:18-22)

As I pondered this powerful event in the life of Moses, God's people had been invited to meet God. Everything seemed to be going just perfectly, until God's people got close enough to the presence of Jehovah!

They were welcomed by **"...thunderings, the lightning flashing, the sound of the trumpet and the mountains smoking."**

What do you do with such an encounter? Well, if you have a guilty conscience, you wouldn't want to draw any closer!

Now, if your mind and hands are pure, you would want to go further and deeper into the mountain and maybe, just maybe, if you are lucky, you would see God face to face!

What people call God's presence today, is nothing more than an emotion stirred by a concert-like atmosphere adorned by flashy lights and proud-hearted musicians giving it their best to be acknowledged by the crowd or the church members.

The Real Presence of God

In Exodus 20, Moses allows us to see what the real presence was like. It was thundering, there was lightning, trumpets sounding, and smoke coming out of the mountains, and the dread of God was felt!

There was so much presence that people feared and trembled!

Does this sound like our modern presence of God? Is this what churches are seeing today? I think not!

The real presence of God brings about a quickening to our hearts. A quickening so powerful that a realization of our true condition before God is exposed!

There is enough power to make a man tremble to the depth of his spiritual marrow of his bones.

To this experience, the children of Israel stood far off.

Here's what they said to Moses, **"You speak with us, and we will hear; but let not God speak with us, lest we die."**

This is a very interesting revelation in that God manifested Himself in this way.

The people knew their own hearts, but didn't want anything to do with God's real presence. They would rather get someone else to vouch for them, to stand up for them. This would be Moses as a mediator.

The bottom line was that they didn't want to die because of God's presence!

God's Presence Will Kill Your Flesh!

When God appears in His glory, it is to kill everything that is not of His nature. To do away with selfishness and anything that would hinder His purpose in your life.

The children of Israel didn't want to deal with self, so they got Moses to communicate via this second-hand revelation.

God specifically told them that God was there to test them; he was there to expose their sin and bring them closer.

No matter what Moses said to them, the people still decided to stay away and have nothing to do with cultivating an intimate walk with Jehovah God!

The real presence of God will always reveal your true condition before God.

I'm sorry to say that God's presence has nothing to do with theatrics, the pastor's fancy footwork, expensive sound systems, and/or luxurious-looking buildings.

His presence has everything to do with His power and purpose for your life!

Neh'enah.

17

Are We Making God Sick?!

"And to the angel of the church of the Laodiceans write, 'These things says the Amen, the Faithful and True Witness, the Beginning of the creation of God: I know your works, that you are neither cold nor hot. I could wish you were cold or hot. So then, because you are lukewarm, and neither cold nor hot, I will vomit you out of My mouth. Because you say, 'I am rich, have become wealthy, and have need of nothing'" "And do not know that you are wretched, miserable, poor, blind, and naked—I counsel you to buy from Me gold refined in the fire, that you may be rich; and white garments, that you may be clothed, that the shame of your nakedness may not be revealed; and anoint your eyes with eyesalve, that you may see. As many as I love, I rebuke and chasten. Therefore be zealous and repent. Behold, I stand at the door and knock. If anyone hears My voice and opens the

door, I will come in to him and dine with him, and he with Me." (Revelation 3:14-20)

As I met the Lord in prayer early this morning, the Spirit of the Lord quickly made me aware of His intent to communicate with me His mind on the condition of a heart that has gone astray from following hard after God.

As I pondered the thoughts of God, I quickly began to evaluate my own condition and how wrong I have been with different attitudes, ideas, ambitions, and processes.

I asked the Lord to search me, just as David did in Psalm 139:23, **"Look deep into my heart, God, and find out everything I am thinking."** (Contemporary English Version)

I believe that this is the responsibility of every servant — to ask God to turn on His lamp in our hearts and to search it out. If we allow Him to do it, He will!

I began to read the Scripture as the Lord invited me into

this deep communion, the verses I found were in Revelation 3, mainly in regard to the Laodicean church found in verses 14 through 20.

Lukewarm Looks Like This!

Apparently, the Lord was not content with the condition nor the spiritual posture of that one church. The Scripture says that God knew their works! So, what exactly did God know?

Well for starters, God knew that the Laodicean church or group was living a lifestyle of indecision. They could not make up their minds if they were going to be hot or cold for the Lord.

It seems to me that this struggle had been going on for some time, and the Lord was not going to put up with it. He states, **"So then, because you are lukewarm, and neither cold nor hot, I will vomit you out of My mouth."**

Lukewarm Attitude Is What?

A lukewarm attitude is a heart that defends its external reputation as it appears to the outside world; it pretends that all things are well, but inwardly it is not.

Only God sees this. The Lord says that the result of living this way, will get you vomited out of His mouth.

That doesn't sound like anything good is going to come out of a lukewarm individual, does it?

For clarity, the word vomit in the original Greek, means to spit. You get the picture.

Have Need of Nothing!

"I am rich, have become wealthy, and have need of nothing..."

Nothing is more damning for a person than to say that

they have no need for anything.

The Laodicean church would console their spiritual coldness by telling themselves they were rich, wealthy, and have no need for anything!

The thought of needing nothing will make God cringe! Nothing is more heart-breaking to God than for someone to say that they "have arrived."

Church, we will always need God!

As long as we live on this side of eternity, Jesus will be our Source for everything. Don't ever forget this, and don't allow yourself to be seduced by a lying spirit into thinking otherwise.

Neh'enah.

18

Breaking the Spirit of Laodicea!

"Because you say, 'I am rich, have become wealthy, and have need of nothing'—and do not know that you are wretched, miserable, poor, blind, and naked—I counsel you to buy from Me gold refined in the fire, that you may be rich..." (Revelation 3:17, 18)

When we think of making God sick due to the way our lifestyle is directed and lived out, we have to also wonder how we can bring pleasure and joy to the heart of God.

In my last devotion, I covered the Laodicean church, and how God was not happy with them, or at least some of the reasons why He would vomit them out of His mouth.

I Know Your Works!

The thing about living out a reckless negligent life before God is that He knows! He knows how we have chosen to think, walk, and act. God was not one bit happy regarding the Laodiceans.

The Laodicean church felt accomplished, in good standing with man, yet God knew it all. They were lukewarm; they only did enough to keep up with the status quo, but that was it!

Talk About Attitude!

The Laodiceans said, **"We are rich and wealthy, and have need of nothing."**

Listen, Church, until we are willing to see the way God sees, we will not know what to do with our lives, ministries, and businesses. We will cave-in in despair and falter in every area of our lives due to the lack of spiritual vitality!

If we never come to the place where we truly evaluate our

hearts, we will not make it! Evaluation done God's way, is acknowledging our true spiritual temperature and having a sincere recognition to our true spiritual state. Not too many know how to do this.

Seeing with the Eyes of the Spirit

"...and do not know that you are wretched, miserable, poor, blind, and naked."

Once we recognize and see with God's eyes, we will now know what to do with our dilemma and make the right changes.

The key is to not fight with the Holy Spirit and deny His convictions. We must be quick to take God's side and agree with Him quickly, just as the Scripture says, **"Reach a settlement quickly with your adversary while you're on the way with him..."** (Matthew 5:25)

Agreeing with God is the key to enter into great possibilities!

Here is what God said about the true state of the Laodiceans…"**you are wretched, miserable, poor, blind, and naked…**"

So, what do we do with this? We ask ourselves the following as God has called it out: Are we wretched? Are we miserable? Are we poor? Are we blind? Are we naked?

Let us do the homework to all that God is pointing out and confess to God of our selfishness and rebellion.

Once we agree with the Holy Spirit, the blood will be present to wash us from our self-centeredness! Once cleansed, I promise you, the river of God will flow like a river!

Neh'enah.

19

He That Is IN Me!

"You are of God, little children, and have overcome them, because He who is in you is greater than he who is in the world." (1 John 4:4)

What an amazing revelation the great Apostle John left us!

If anyone at any time and at any place needed affirmation, they will find it in this one powerful verse: **"You are of God!"**

I think often, if believers get lost in the fight then they will lack the perspective and vision of who they truly are.

Most believers who struggle in life do not struggle because the enemy is more powerful, but rather because the believer doesn't know what has been made available to them as far as the weapons of our warfare.

When the mercy of God was revealed to you and I, it was with the intent of God that we who had believed, would live impregnated lives...impregnated by the glorious Spirit of the living God!

John doesn't stop there, listen to the rest of this: **"Little children, you have overcome them."**
In other words, because we are of God, we can overcome. We can potentially win every battle that we will ever have on this side of eternity. Amazing!

Megaton Power!

Then this one part, **"...because He who is in you is greater than he who is in the world."**

Did you hear this? **"He who is IN you is greater!"** Do you truly understand this?

The megaton power that you need to win every battle is

inside you! No need to be whining, complaining, calling people to pray for you, or calling the Christian hotline for deliverance! No! Jesus is more than enough! Learn to Tap-In! Tap into the glory!

Unleashing Christ Through You...

Here is what happens once this revelation becomes the living bread to your spirit— you get bold and full of authority from on high.

In Jesus, position is everything. However big your revelation of Christ is, is how much authority you carry, and how much power you will potentially have to overcome your battles!

As you walk in the revelation that CHRIST IS IN YOU — you will get downloads of wisdom, knowledge, power, and the ability to fight strategically and wisely accompanied by accurate timing! To Him be the glory! Neh'enah.

20

The Wisdom of Saying, NO!

"Then the kingdom of heaven shall be likened to ten virgins who took their lamps and went out to meet the bridegroom. Now five of them were wise, and five were foolish. Those who were foolish took their lamps and took no oil with them, but the wise took oil in their vessels with their lamps. But while the bridegroom was delayed, they all slumbered and slept. And at midnight a cry was heard: Behold, the bridegroom is coming; go out to meet him! Then all those virgins arose and trimmed their lamps. And the foolish said to the wise, Give us some of your oil, for our lamps are going out.' But the wise answered, saying, 'No.'" (Matthew 25:1-9)

The parable mentioned above, has everything to do with making the right choice. I believe all of us have this challenge.

We all have to decide on one thing or another; either we follow what is right and proper, or we follow something that will not lead us to good results.

If you have lived long enough, you have lived enough to see both sides of this.

You have known the blessings of the Lord when things were done according to His plan, and you have tasted the bitterness when things have been done for selfish gain.

If you read the text, you will discover that there were ten virgins. The Bible says that five of those virgins were wise, and the other five were foolish.

The issue here had to do with having enough oil for the lampstand. The wise prepared with sufficient oil; the foolish did not prepare enough oil.

The Wise Know When to Say, No!

Now, when the Bridegroom appeared, the foolish said to

the wise, **"Give us some of your oil, for our lamps are going out."** But the wise answered, saying , 'No.'"

Preparation could have been what the foolish were lacking in their lives, and thus, they paid for it. They sowed laziness, and they reaped nothing!

The real challenge for believers, in my estimation, is knowing when to say no.

I think this is more a matter of character than anything else.

Many times, our futures have been altered because of bad decisions we have made. We should have said, no, but we didn't think it through, and usually end-up paying for it in the future.

The wise are wise because they know when to act, how to act, and where to act. Saying no something or someone is not a bad thing, if the end result will bring stability and assurance to both parties.

Sometimes saying no is necessary because of dangers ahead; possible pain and hurt might be at the other end. Loss of finances and friendships are also weighing in the balance.

In closing this meditation, I believe that we should always aim to be wise. Being wise is the mind that says, **"If I say yes – what will be the result of my decision? Will it bring pain, or will it bring joy?"**

Neh'enah.

21

No Room for Two!

"So Moses finished the work. Then the cloud covered the tabernacle of meeting, and the glory of the Lord filled the tabernacle. And Moses was not able to enter the tabernacle of meeting, because the cloud rested above it, and the glory of the Lord filled the tabernacle." (Exodus 40:33-35)

What an interesting portion I discovered this morning as I waited upon the Lord's wisdom...

Moses was commanded by the Lord to construct a tabernacle in the wilderness, a meeting place, if you will, where God would meet man and instruct him. To all this, Moses kept the command and proceeded to build this Tabernacle.

Much work went into it, and finally Exodus 40:33 tells us

that, **"...Moses finished the work."**

After Moses completed the tabernacle by arranging everything in its proper place, a strange phenomenon took place — the glory of the Lord descended upon it and went into this man-made skin-covered tent!

It says, **"Then the cloud covered the tabernacle of meeting, and the glory of the Lord filled the tabernacle."** Can you picture this?

Room for Only One!

The Scripture goes on to say that, **"Moses was not able to enter the tabernacle of meeting, because the cloud rested above it, and the glory of the Lord filled the tabernacle."**

What was this all about? Why couldn't Moses enter in? Why could he not experience the very promise he had just constructed? It left me with many thoughts as I continued to pray....

Then the Lord spoke to my heart and said, *"David, when I ask man to carry out My wishes, it is always for my good pleasure, not man's pleasure. Anything I send My word to accomplish, it is always all for Me! My glory will always outshine everything around it!"* Enough said.

Lessons from Moses' Encounter

The first lesson is this: Order must precede His presence in our lives. We cannot expect God to move in us and through us when we are living in outright rebellion and disobedience. God may be merciful at times, but it is not normal for God to use a dirty vessel.

Once Moses set the tabernacle in godly order – then the glory came down and went inside to fill it. Do you see this?

The second lesson is this: Once the glory of the Lord is present, man must decrease. Just get out of God's way – this is all about God and what He desires to accomplish through His glory!

Too often, man wants to blend in with His presence, but I have learned that we are nothing more than God's servants to do His bidding, not ours! We are called to build according to His idea and detail and then say, "It is finished Lord."

Once He sees it done – He will proceed to do things that will bring Him pleasure and joy!

Great words came from John the Baptist, **"He must increase, but I must decrease."** (John 3:30)

Neh'enah.

22

And the Glory of the Lord Will Appear!

"So they brought what Moses commanded before the tabernacle of meeting. And all the congregation drew near and stood before the Lord. Then Moses said, 'This is the thing which the Lord commanded you to do, and the glory of the Lord will appear to you.'" (Leviticus 9:5-6)

Is it really that complicated to keep up with the Lord's plan and purpose for our lives?

Sometimes, it can surely feel like this— other times, it feels very do-able. I have experienced the gentleness of God in my life, and I have also partaken in resisting God's will for my life (and to my shame) way too many times to count.

God is a God of Order!

The Lord's will is already pre-designed. He knows exactly what He wants to do with our life. He created you and I for such a time as this. We weren't created so we could run our own enterprise apart from His heart.

If anything of impact is going to happen in our lives – it will be on His terms and in His timing.

I hear too many believers say, "I want to see revival like the old days!"

My question back to them is, "Are we positioned [spiritually-speaking] like the days of old?"

Are we appropriating the pattern that brings such fire and glory to our life, our ministry, our business, and our ventures? I think this would be a good place to start evaluating the why of why so little happens in our lives.

If we refuse to follow a godly format, pattern or plan – our selfish plans will come to nothing. They will be short-lived at best!

"This is the Thing!"

Moses brought God's people near and said to them, **"This is the thing which the Lord commanded you to do, and the glory of the Lord will appear to you."**

If you do a bit of reading into the Scriptures before these, they speak of Israel offering sacrifices along with the priests. If this was to be followed, Moses said that they would see the glory of the Lord.

It is usually one thing that always hinders us from entering into greater fullness in God.

I believe God has great things for all who believe.

Some love to hear only God. Others love to obey God but with no instruction. Now, there are other servants of God, they love to hear and then obey God's plan. Which one are you?

I remember A.W. Tozer wrote a book many years ago, entitled God Tells the Man Who Cares. I figured this: If God is taking the time to share the secrets that will empower my life, I then must follow His plans and see His glory!

What you live out is what you believe. If God has a plan for you, He will unfold it. He will also download the details of it, so that you may experience His glory and power!

Neh'enah.

23

The Father Knows Your Need!

"When they had twisted a crown of thorns, they put it on His head, and a reed in His right hand. And they bowed the knee before Him and mocked Him, saying, 'Hail, King of the Jews!' Then they spat on Him and took the reed and struck Him on the head. And when they had mocked Him, they took the robe off Him, put His own clothes on Him, and led Him away to be crucified. Now as they came out, they found a man of Cyrene, Simon by name. Him they compelled to bear His cross." (Matthew 27:29-32)

In reading this passage, I came across a very interesting point. Let me share a few things that will encourage your heart and quicken your mind for your faith journey.

While reading these few passages, I came across a passage

that has always made me wonder. It has always made me think to myself, Why this random act?

By this time, Jesus had been severely beaten and now was at the stage where the soldiers had made a crown of thorns and had placed it on His head, and with a mocking spirit, proceeded to say, "Hail King of the Jews!"

If you have watched any movies on the life of Jesus, for me, it has always been very difficult to see the whole crucifixion through. Too painful to watch and too heart-wrenching to endure! I usually fast forward this event.

Anyhow, after they dressed him up, and they sent Him away to be crucified. Many scholars say that by this time, Jesus was almost dead. The beatings, the abuse, and now the burden of carrying His cross to Calvary – it was too much for a man to handle– and the Father knew it!

A Man with a Mission!

There is no doubt in my mind, that Jesus was a man with a mission. He embodied the idea of God's purpose. Yet in following the Father's will, it was not an easy thing.

As a matter of fact, following the Father's heart would cost Him everything and the Father knew it!

Anyone who decides to follow God with all their might, will always face difficulty. It will get difficult as one proceeds to pierce the darkness. Yet, for all this, God will always make provisions. Glory to God!

While Jesus is facing all the abuse and a torture, the Father is taking note. He is not going to bail out on anything.

The Father knew that Jesus would be so beaten and so impacted emotionally, spiritually and physically that even to the end, the Father would be right there to take His Son Jesus all the way through!

Supernatural Favor & Provision!

As Jesus begins the long journey to Calvary, He is obviously too weak to carry the heavy cross.

It is usually this way for any serious servant of God who is making the effort to please the Father with their lives.

It is at this time, as we are pursuing the heart of God, that God's supernatural favor reveals itself.

Just as things had become very difficult and almost next to impossible in His natural strength to get to the place the Father had prepared for Him, a man by the name of Simon was told to help Jesus carry the heavy cross.

This is the way God provides for us!

This is the way the Father has it all outlined. He will ask us to do something and along the way, He will raise up people smarter, wiser, and stronger than us, so we can get the job done!

One thing I have learned from this meditation: If anyone

walks in God's plan, in God's will – the Lord Himself, will provide all we need to get to the finish line!

So, if you are going through discouragement today, or if things are not looking very good for you…. don't fret. Your "Simon" is just around the corner!

Neh'enah.

24

Learn to Live by His Wishes Not Only His Laws!

"Now in the morning, having risen a long while before daylight, He went out and departed to a solitary place; and there He prayed." (Mark 1:35)

This morning, I had a tremendous inspirational moment. As I meditated upon the last year, I started to evaluate much of what has transpired in my life and ministry.

I was reminded of the words from a man I heard speak years ago at some conference or seminar: He said, "You are where you are, because that is the place you have chosen to be!"

As I pondered these words and revisited my present state of mind and heart, I realized that I can vouch for this man's

"prophetic" statement. It is true!
Some things I like and have taken pleasure in; other things, I am not very content with. Many would say, "Well, that is life!"

I get all that, but somehow and in some way, I am not wired that way. I'm not one to stand still and watch the world pass by.

Maybe you are the type of individual who believes that God is going to do everything for you: pay your bills, change your flat tire, spoon feed you, and make the choices for you. If you believe that, you are in for a rude awakening! I'm just saying.

God Is Not in Control!

For years, I have heard people make this proclamation, "God is in control, brother!"

I used to reply with a big, "Amen" to this. Until I grew up!

The Lord has granted you and I (who have come into His kingdom) the power and the authority to live His life on earth.

His life entails: wisdom, knowledge, authority, power, a sound mind, an awakened spirit, and the good favor of God. Not to mention the countless ideas and abilities to carry out ALL His wishes! Do you agree?

Maybe You Need New Tires!

I'll never forget when I heard a dear brother say, "I woke up this morning and was getting ready to go to church and noticed that one of the tires of my car was flat."

I said to myself, "The Devil doesn't want me to go to church."

So, I found a way to get to church by getting a ride with someone else."

As I sat there and listened to this spiritual kindergarten individual, I said to myself, "I can just picture Satan himself, leaving his worldwide wicked agenda and coming down to Alton, Texas to puncture the tire of this dear brother!" Yeah. No! How insane is this thought!

As he shared his deep revelation with the congregation, I also had a revelation: I felt like saying, "Maybe it's not Satan who punctured your tire. Perhaps you just need new tires!"

Whatever we feed our minds and hearts is the kind of leadership we will follow.

If all we have in our heads are selfish thoughts, then we will think selfishly and act selfishly.

If we allow God to fill us with His heart, then we will do things accordingly to His heart.

Let's Stop Living in a Spiritual Fantasy!

Get in touch with the Spirit of God on a daily basis. Learn from God! Let Him speak His will in fullness to you. Lend yourself to the Lord so that you may appropriate His promises. Learn to live by His wishes, not only His laws!

Neh'enah.

25

It's Really Not About the Institution!

Here goes one of my meditations that I have been pondering for some time now.

The other day, while speaking to an individual at the coffee shop, he shared with me his disinterest with the institution that I call church.

He proceeded to say that churches were full of hypocrites, and that the preachers or pastors were only money-grabbers! Ouch.

I thought to myself, this guy is on a roll. Where should I stop him? Or should I let him speak his mind? Well, I decided to let him have his rant. He went on and on about how imperfect it was and so forth...you can just imagine.

I learned some great things from this one particular individual.

At first it makes sense to blame the institution, but as you ponder more deeply, you will discover that you only get what you are looking for.

Let a Baby Teach Us!

Take a baby for example. The baby is content by having a bottle, being changed when they need to be changed, and a small crib will accommodate them just fine. At this stage, all is well.

The baby then grows a bit more. One bottle is not enough, and being changed is happening at a faster rate. The small crib stops being accommodating, and now they desire more space.

Sooner than later, the baby grows and grows that now, a room is needed for this little toddler to find joy. They have a myriad of toys and want to play with them. A room is required. Do you get the point?

As we grow on a personal level, our environment must grow as well. As people grow, they require space. Too often the space is not provided. What can one do?

Providing that you are not angry or bitter towards someone due to a bad transaction, experience, or are carrying any envy, jealousy, or discord in your heart, transitioning should not be hard.

You Get What You Are!

My philosophy in life is a basic one: You get what you are! Whether it be the institution of the family, government, church, business, or any type of corporation, it is always human led. Whoever it is that leads these institutions – will play a big role to its outcome.

The institution provides a setting for you to find what you are looking for. Once you find it, you will enjoy it. How long you enjoy this ride is contingent upon your development. As you develop, the demands grow.

The institution is not there to accommodate you, but as you develop in the institution, you become part of its growing process.

Take the illustration of the baby for example: The baby gets to the development stage where they become a teenager. They no longer need their mom to give them a bottle - if they are hungry, they will open the refrigerator!

There will come a time when you will have to help yourself!

Development and Growth

Development and growth are things that happen in an institution. Some grow faster than others— yet others, grow according to their leader. If you are growing faster than your leaders, you might be having to change the environment very soon.

I think it's wise to meet with that leader and voice your concern for growth and development.

I Can't Get No Satisfaction

Too often, the sign of dissatisfaction comes upon us. We are no longer feeling the emotion of how things used to be. We are no longer running to the institution, but rather running away from it! Has this happened to you?

Dissatisfaction is a sign that things have changed or shifted; we better find out what has changed and why are we feeling this way. These two things are key.

Deep Introspection and Evaluation

What is happening in you? Are you blaming the institution for your personal stagnation? Are you blaming an individual for your lack of development? Are you mad at someone for short-changing you? Are they to blame? Are you to blame?

Before making any major moves, shifts, relocations, or re-positionings, it would be wise to do introspection first. Evaluate your present state. Where were you yesterday? Where are you today? Where do you want to be tomorrow? If one can answer these questions, you can pretty much find your way through any transition.

It's Nobody's Fault!

I know that sometimes it is easier to blame someone else for our misfortune, our challenges, our adversities, etc.

Yet, in light of spiritual development, it would be to our advantage to always look inward first. Find out what God is doing and saying and then move accordingly.

Neh'enah.

26

It Is What You Make It!

"...but one thing I do, forgetting those things which are behind and reaching forward to those things which are ahead, I press toward the goal for the prize of the up-ward call of God in Christ Jesus." (Philippians 3:13, 14)

As we near the end of yet another year in the cycle of life, I have heard the heart of many friends, acquaintances and colleagues say, "I wonder what the New Year has in store for us?"

Many of them are looking into the future with great confi-dence, while others are a bit uncertain. Yet, there are those who did not have a good past year and feel to some degree fear.

Actually, this morning at the coffee shop, a man approached me and said, "This year is almost over. I hope next year brings us good things and greater opportunities."

Then he proceeded to ask me, "What do you make of it?" I quietly leaned over to him so that I would not embarrass him and quietly said to him, "The future has to do with you. It will be what you make it to be!"

I truly believe this philosophy of life. Life will be whatever you make it to be.

Be the Best Steward You Can Be!

The Lord Himself provides life. He gives strength, ability to act, think, and speak. Yes, the Lord provides all the elements for us to bring glory to His Name. The Lord Himself is the One who releases ambition, vision, and the power to carry it out. This part is all God's.

The stewardship part comes in when we make the choice to build upon all the blocks God has given us.

We either build or we don't build.

To say for the sake of sounding pious or noble, "God will lead me," or "I will see what the Lord has in store for me," have to be some of the shallowest comments I have heard from so called Christians.

Either they don't know that God has already provided all things for us to be successful or they are parroting some preacher somewhere who is trying to sound "religious."

The fact is that Christ has made a way for us to enter into His kingdom, which happens to be the bedrock of God's original intent for humanity. In it, you will find: delegated authority, true identity, power to carry out His wishes, and greatness by serving others.

If you are not walking in delegated authority, in true identity, in God's perfect will, or becoming more and more like Jesus by serving others, then obviously something is missing!

Don't lose focus: **"Jesus has paved the way for you and I to live an abundant life."** (John 10:10)

I will conclude by saying, you don't have to be afraid of your future! Remember: "The future belongs to those who create it!"

Neh'enah.

27

Come Away and Rest!

"Then the apostles gathered to Jesus and told Him all things, both what they had done and what they had taught. And He said to them, 'Come aside by yourselves to a deserted place and rest a while.' For there were many coming and going, and they did not even have time to eat." (Mark 6:30, 31)

This past year has been filled with many challenges. Whether I was faced with spiritual, physical or emotional challenges, all would find their cure in coming away and finding rest in the arms of God.

This usually happens to people who are driven and long to make a difference in their world. The temptation to go and go without proper rest to replenish one's spirit in God, is an all too common trap for the human soul.

Way Too Busy!

But let us take some time to do some introspection; let us evaluate why our lives start to dwindle emotionally, spiritually, and finally physically.

As I sit here at the coffee shop, I see the daily hustle and bustle. People run in and get their coffee, and then run out, get in their cars and head off to their destination.

I believe it is very easy to get caught up in our work, our goals, and our vision. Ambition for the most part, seems to be the driving force.

To some degree, I believe these things should be in place and we should be zealous with our life goals. I am in no way suggesting a lazy apathetic lifestyle!

What Is Valuable to You?

This brings me up to my next point: What is valuable to

you? For people who have never tasted the Lord's goodness, who have never experienced the powers of the age that is to come —life seems pretty cut and dry. It is all about materialism, where more is better and tangibility must be the order of the day.

Is it important to watch your hard work manifest itself? Absolutely. I think everyone should enjoy the fruits of their labor.

The Secret Element

Now, there is one thing that sets those who know God apart from those who don't. It's a spiritual government.

Spiritual government is God's ability to direct your steps. It's that part that says, "Go ahead and make your plans, but I the Lord, will order them!"

Without this element in your life, you are just floating in an ocean full of uncertainty. Your sails might be up, but where are you heading? What is your destination? It's a scary feeling not knowing where all this will end up.

If you allow God to be your everything, your life will never lack peace, joy or spiritual government [direction.]

Don't burn out! "Come aside by yourselves to a deserted place and rest a while."

It is the intention of God to walk with you every step of the way in your personal life, business, ministry, and any endeavor you set yourself to accomplish. Dwell on this deeply.

Neh'enah.

28

Can You Tell It Is Him? - Part 1

"Immediately He made His disciples get into the boat and go before Him to the other side, to Bethsaida, while He sent the multitude away. And when He had sent them away, He departed to the mountain to pray. Now when evening came, the boat was in the middle of the sea; and He was alone on the land. Then He saw them straining at rowing, for the wind was against them. Now about the fourth watch of the night He came to them, walking on the sea, and would have passed them by. And when they saw Him walking on the sea, they supposed it was a ghost, and cried out; for they all saw Him and were troubled. But immediately He talked with them and said to them, 'Be of good cheer! It is I; do not be afraid.' Then He went up into the boat to them, and the wind ceased. And they were greatly amazed in themselves beyond measure, and marveled. For they had not understood

about the loaves, because their heart was hardened." (Mark 6:45-52)

Faith Must Increase!

One of the things that I have come to know in my walk with God, is the way He tests our lives and brings us to higher ground. Obviously, it is the Lord's heart and will to refine us and bring us into His likeness.
Any invitation from the Lord, I venture say, has this end in mind. The Scripture says, **"Immediately He made His disciples get into the boat and go before Him to the other side..."**

Why the urgency? Why the push to get into the boat?

I think it is the way the Lord works with His disciples. He gives us no time to think things through. Yes, faith is not something you think and decide; faith is something you immediately know and act upon!

One must know that every invitation coming from God is for the purpose of growing and expanding in faith.

I have heard people sometimes boast of how God called them into ministry or into some venture. Once they jump in, they quickly are met with the challenges of that ministry or venture.

A tremendous jolt into their character is felt quickly and decisions must be made: Should I continue? Should I quit?

Testing Is Inevitable!

Now, some people don't want to be tested. Some people don't want to grow in God! They would rather let others do the growing up, while they play the religious game of being saved.

One thing is sure: Those who want to grow in God will be tested.

For all who desire to go deeper into the things of the Lord – know that you will have to face the floods of testing and not just the fiery darts of the enemy!

I have come to know that Christ's friendly invitations are always related to some character-forming experience.

Neh'enah.

29

Can You Tell It Is Him? - Part 2

"Now about the fourth watch of the night He came to them, walking on the sea, and would have passed them by. And when they saw Him walking on the sea, they supposed it was a ghost, and cried out; for they all saw Him and were troubled." (Mark 6:48-50)

It's a Ghost!

As we dive into the text, we will discover that Jesus sent the disciples ahead. Then the Scripture says something very unique: **"He departed to the mountain to pray."**

I guess my question would be, why did He depart to pray? I really don't know, but I do have a theory.

I believe Jesus knew that the disciples were to be tested,

and , He had probably talked to the Father about it.

Perhaps Jesus said to the Father, "I'm going to test them in the realm of faith. Father, don't let them fail this one test. This is going to be one of those lifelong tests that they will have to go through over and over again as they walk in my kingdom here on earth."

Then it happened.

The Word says, **"Then He saw them straining at rowing, for the wind was against them."**

It is clear to me that the Lord invites us to come into His realm for an experience, but then waits for our natural strength to come to an end, before He steps in. Such a classic move from the Lord. Listen closely…

"And when they saw Him walking on the sea, they supposed it was a ghost, and cried out; for they all saw Him and were troubled."

How can this be? How can He be a ghost? I mean, I know He is walking on water; this is enough to send anyone on a tailspin, but hadn't they seen Him do miracles before? Had they not sat and ate with Him before?

I know they had sat before Him and heard His teachings. So, what was the problem? Or better yet, where is God's test in this scenario?

Discerning Christ in the Spirit-Man.

The real test comes to us when we are challenged to recognize Christ in our spirit-man. Unless we see Him in our hearts, we are not truly seeing Him!

Too often Christians have this mental image of Jesus Christ – they see Him as this handsome looking Jewish man with a nice beard and fancy outer garment. Though this may be the case, Christ must also be discerned in the spirit-man.

Our natural faculties more often than not, get the best of

us.

If things don't appear as we think they should, we go into a panic. We get nervous when our natural eyes don't see Jesus as we have known Him in the past.

The whole test here was that the disciples would get a glimpse of Christ in their inner-man, their spirit-man!

All of God's tests have to do with our spiritual advancement and nothing else. Unless our hearts are captured by His beauty, we won't see it!

Be of Good Cheer! It is I.

Finally, Jesus discloses Himself to the disciples.

It was a must for Christ to do this otherwise they would have been filled with fear. Christ literally had to dumb-it down for the disciples to recognize His presence.

You see, when our hearts are hardened, clouded, or filled

with the preconceived ideas of yesterday, we may just miss Him altogether!

Let us humble ourselves with every invitation coming from the Lord. We must understand that He is unto something that will affect our spiritual development.

Humility will unlock every secret for the servant of God.

Neh'enah.

30

Don't Abort God's Dream!

"He hath made everything beautiful in his time..." (Ecclesiastes 3:11 KJV)

We always teach people to believe in God's miraculous power; to not doubt. We encourage people to hold on to God's faithfulness and endure hardships like good soldiers.

Yes, it seems to be the religious thing to simply be positive about everything in life and just trust God with everything.

I trust God with every outcome, and even when I lack understanding, I tend to hold on to His sovereignty and just believe. I'm sure you have experienced the same.

God's Method

In the midst of all the hype of having faith in God, many believers become disillusioned because their prayers are not being answered in the midst of a fiery furnace of testing.

Nothing tests the heart and resolve of a believer more than feeling abandoned by friends, family, and even God. It's an incredible feeling of loneliness as the Lord squeezes the life out of His servants.

Many believers today question this method. They will ask, "Will God allow this to happen to me, His child?"

The answer is: Yes!

Nothing gets the dross out of the gold like God's fire. Just listen to this: **"So that the proof of your faith, being more precious than gold which is perishable, even though tested by fire, may be found to result in praise and glory and honor at the revelation of Jesus Christ..."** (1 Peter

1:7) God is using fire to mature us!

God's Process

Now, the process.

God's process of working in our lives is unique. His testing is usually based on the development of character. It is not a true or false test; it's not a fill in the blank test; it's not based on past experience or religious knowledge. God's tests are based on decisions made at the right time and with the right motives!

Everything about you and I will be tested. This will include – attitudes, motives, decisions, actions, commitment, humility, and how we handle circumstances in our lives.

Why So Long?

God is always working in our lives. It seems like an endless work of teaching and breaking and teaching and breaking. As hard as it may seem, it is inevitable. God must accomplish His perfect work in us.

Don't look for shortcuts. Don't look for favors. Don't look for a friend to bail you out. I repeat: Allow the Lord to do His perfect work in you!

A Word of Caution

Many years ago, a very good prophetic friend of mine sent me an email with an interesting story. As I close this meditation, I would like to share this revelation with you. The story goes something like this:

A lady went to a park one Sunday afternoon. She sat on a bench, which by the way, was surrounded by beautiful trees, and even some branches hung over the bench where this lady was sitting. While the lady looked on and saw kids playing, she also noticed that on one of the branches sat a cocoon. She noticed how this butterfly-to-be was fighting to break out of this cocoon. Feeling much compassion for this poor helpless and weak butterfly, the lady decided to help this poor thing by opening the cocoon herself to the place where this butterfly could just get out with hardly any effort. The butterfly, which was still undeveloped, made her way out of the cocoon and dropped to the ground. She couldn't fly much less defend herself from any ants or bugs that would eventually kill her. End of story.

What can we learn?

If God is not letting you out of the cocoon of testing yet, it is probably because you are not fully developed yet and you don't have wings to fly.

Don't be in a hurry to get out and fly. You don't have wings yet!

You will know when it's time to fly because God will tell you. You see, **"He makes all things beautiful in His time."**

Wait for His time. Your turn is coming up!

Neh'enah.

31

God's Formula for Miracles!

"Now in the morning, as they passed by, they saw the fig tree dried up from the roots. And Peter, remembering, said to Him, 'Rabbi, look! The fig tree which You cursed has withered away.' So, Jesus answered and said to them, 'Have faith in God. For assuredly, I say to you, whoever says to this mountain, "Be removed and be cast into the sea," and does not doubt in his heart, but believes that those things he says will be done, he will have whatever he says. Therefore, I say to you, whatever things you ask when you pray, believe that you receive them, and you will have them.'" (Mark 11:20-24)

It's time for you to see miracles in your life or should I say, "It's time to make the supernatural, natural."

In other words, miracles are not miracles – what people call miracles are actually manifestations of how things really look in the heavenly realm.

From God's perspective, it is normal to see alignment take place. Yet, people get wowed when they see a miracle.

When one catches a glimpse of God's dimension, and I mean only a glimpse (as small as a mustard seed) so-called miracles will take place here on earth.
You Can Do Them!

I have come to know a bit of this world of miracles in my own life.

To see miracles and get wowed by them is so normal for believers, yet when you actually learn the secret of releasing God's power on earth by the revelation of what He gives to your heart, then faith is activated and what people call "miracles" take place!

A Miracle at the Rehab Center

A couple of weeks ago I was asked if I could go and pray

for a brother at a rehab center. I made my way to visit him and just as I thought, the dear brother was in distress and waiting upon God for some miracle to come his way.

I proceeded to sit and talk with him about his illness and the doctor's prognosis, etc.

His diabetes seemed to be under control, but his eyesight was not good. He was seeing double. I told him that God had a great plan and knowing the way God tends to work in our lives, I suggested for him to take this time at the rehab as a season where he needed to rest and wait upon the Lord.

He seemed to take my counsel and began to cry in desperation of what was happening to him. I told him that I would pray for him before I would leave.

I took his hands and held them as I prayed and prophesied over his life. I told him that God was going to give him vision for 2020. He needed this time to find God's will, and I told him specifically that in 72 hours (3 days) his vision would return to normal. I said amen and left the facility.

A few days later, while I was at the bank, this man called me back. He told me that what I had prophesied about his vision returning in 72 hours, had just happened. He was in tears and thankful to God for His endless mercy!

I saw it in my spirit, and I spoke it over him without doubting. Just as the Scripture says, **"...whatever things you ask when you pray, believe that you receive them, and you will have them."**

God Is Not Joking!

What I saw, I believed and knew in my heart that God would answer me according to my request.

I believe God will do the same for you.

Here's the formula to God's endless miracles:
Hear or see, what God is saying or revealing;
Believe that you have received (what you heard or saw)

when you requested; You will have it, if you don't doubt!

Neh'enah.

32

It's Your Time to Arise!

"After the death of Moses the servant of the Lord, it came to pass that the Lord spoke to Joshua the son of Nun, Moses' assistant, saying: 'Moses My servant is dead. Now therefore, arise, go over this Jordan, you and all this people, to the land which I am giving to them—the children of Israel. Every place that the sole of your foot will tread upon I have given you, as I said to Moses.'" (Joshua 1:1-3)

In my meditation this morning, I was reflecting on the words that the Lord gave Joshua as he became the leader of God's people. Can you imagine this picture?

For starters, Moses had died. Things looked pretty grim, and I'm almost sure everyone was bathed in sorrow and grief. Yet, the call of God to progress was ever before them.

Now Joshua, was a man of war and was now taking full responsibility of God's people as their primary leader. Indeed, Joshua was undertaking a huge task— nevertheless, God was with him every step of the way!

I venture to say that if God is in charge, it will make the difference in any situation with anyone who is willing to walk and be led by His Spirit.

Moses Is Dead!

I have noticed that many obstacles are present, and they tend to surround us at various times.

Obstacles come in degrees: for example, some obstacles are small hurdles to cross, but some are tormenting and tend to cling or drag longer.

Whether it be a physical, emotional or a spiritual obstacle – it must be detected, discerned, and subdued through the precious blood of Jesus! We must move in the power that works mightily in us.

I'm sure Joshua was grieving for his spiritual father Moses when the Lord came to him and said, **"Moses My servant is dead. Now therefore, arise, go over this Jordan..."**

So much for comprehension, understanding, and sympathy coming from the Lord. It was God's words to Joshua saying, "Ok Joshua, get over it! It's time to move forward. All this grieving is not going to get us across the Jordan – so arise and go!"

It has been my experience that when confronted with a crisis, an obstacle, or some difficult situation, the Holy Spirit will always bring us back to God's original intent.

Why did we start marching towards the Promised Land? Why did we start this or that? Nothing like getting yourself situated in God's original intent.

If We Obey . . .

Not only must we align ourselves with God's original intent, but we must also follow instruction for the next chapter in our venture.

The Lord told Joshua, **"Every place that the sole of your foot will tread upon I have given you, as I said to Moses."**

When we align our attitude with God's original plan or intent, revelation will come.

Nothing clouds God's revelation more than a wrong attitude towards negative situations.

I have come to learn that God speaks in an orderly fashion to those who care to listen and follow.

He will first ask us to do one thing— and as we do it, He will proceed to give us another thing to do. The second thing is usually always contingent upon the first thing.

Please make a note of this as you pursue God's original intent for your own life, ministry, and business. Neh'enah.

33

Faith Jumps! Fear Looks!

"And every one of you came near to me and said, 'Let us send men before us, and let them search out the land for us, and bring back word to us of the way by which we should go up, and of the cities into which we shall come.' The plan pleased me well; so I took twelve of your men, one man from each tribe. And they departed and went up into the mountains, and came to the Valley of Eshcol, and spied it out. They also took some of the fruit of the land in their hands and brought it down to us; and they brought back word to us, saying, 'It is a good land which the Lord our God is giving us.' Nevertheless, you would not go up, but rebelled against the command of the Lord your God..." (Deuteronomy 1:22-26)

Today I want to bring forth this meditation on the subject of faith.

Everything that has to do with the Lord requires faith.

It requires faith to know that He is; it requires faith to know that He will act; it requires faith to believe that what you have seen in your heart, is truly a picture that God has drawn; and it takes faith to know with the most of deepest assurance, that it will manifest itself in due time!

A Land That Flows with Milk and Honey

God painted a picture in the minds and hearts of God's people. The picture had to do with abundance and prosperity.

The Lord promised His children that if they would obey Him, they would eat the good of the land.

The challenge was for God's people, for them to believe in all that God had promised.

Obviously, by reading the story, we see how God's people failed miserably in this venture.

God was trying to bring His people into a land that flowed with blessings— a land that they would inhabit and settle with their families.

God's people had a destiny, and they threw it all away! Why? No faith.

When God Speaks It Is as Good as Done!

Every revelation from the Lord, every promise from God – they are all contingent upon our faith to believe what He has said.

By faith we apprehend every promise from the Lord. We must first believe, then we must act.

After we believe what God says, we must then act with holy fear. We can't entertain the uncertainties, the obstacles, or even the lack of resources, to get to where God desires to take us.

God's people were doubting God's promise, so they requested proof of how good the land was.

Moses chose twelve spies and sent them out to spy out the land for forty days. The spies came back with a great report of their findings…the land was awesome!

Yet, there were obstacles standing in the way – there were giants in the land. Seeing and hearing this, the people doubted and refused to go into their promise.

It's About Cooperation!

The Lord always wants to be the leader in everything He tells you to do. He doesn't need your resources; He only needs our cooperation!

When we begin to think that we have to do this or that, we have already missed God's plan for increase in our lives.

The idea is: God speaks to us first, then we agree. We then act on what He instructs us and when He tells us to act. Let your mind dwell on these thoughts. Neh'enah.

34

Lord, Sign Me Up!

"Also, I heard the voice of the Lord, saying:
"Whom shall I send,
And who will go for Us?"
Then I said, "Here am I! Send me." (Isaiah 6:8)

I want to start by saying that it has been my experience to see how in the kingdom of God, certain demands are placed on every citizen. The demand that comes from the King is to follow Him, His decrees, precepts, and laws.

For the most part, kingdom citizens desire what the King desires. Whatever those desires may be, citizens are almost always ready to keep and to follow.

Being in the Right Place

The right place for kingdom citizens, is to see themselves as sons and daughters to the King. To be in good standing with the King is key to His favor.

If there is no alignment, then serving the King will be a struggle and it will not be enjoyable. There is nothing worse than trying to follow God and and to be hating it every step of the way!

Once the citizen understands that it is all about positioning oneself under the Lordship of the King, (not to mention a heart full of disposition and willingness to please Him at any cost) immeasurable joy will overtake that citizen.

For the most part, citizens follow the King without trying very hard; it's more a matter of trust.

If one doesn't trust the King with their life or their future – they will end up defaulting into trying extremely hard to make life happen.

Here I Am!

Part of being a citizen is that the King may have special work for you. God will come to you and awaken your spirit; He will vivify what He instilled in you before you were ever born.

These desires that have been dormant in you will awaken, and then you will really start living.

If one is trying very hard to make life happen, they will have to depend upon their success to feel validated, appreciated and accepted.

If one trusts the King with every area of His life and they know in their hearts that all things will turn out just as the King has previously shown them, then one can rest.
Resting in the facts is better than running after an illusion.

Changed!

Isaiah saw the Lord high and lifted up! He was moved deeply. His spirit was awakened to the reality of God, his soul was consumed with unworthiness, and his body wanted to run and hide!

Yet in all of this, God had an awesome plan for Isaiah. To release Him into a greater fullness of his destiny.

The plan was laid out, the invitation was given, but Isaiah had to make a decision.

Only Isaiah had the key to his destiny. Please note: It wasn't until Isaiah said, "Here am I, send me," that the key to his destiny was unlocked.

It is not enough knowing about it or reading about it. The key must be placed in the keyhole, and the door must open for destiny to flow in you.

Keep this in mind: You will suffer in some way in this life, no matter what you do. You can suffer in God's will or you can suffer outside of God's will. We will make that choice.

I don't know about you, but I would one-million times over, rather suffer under God's order than to suffer doing my own thing!

When Isaiah said, **"Here am I, send me,"** the doors were split wide open and now God could have His way in this vessel; yes, and this vessel now had the favor of God upon his life!

Was Isaiah's life easier after this encounter—I don't really know. What I do know, is this: Isaiah lived out his life doing the will of Jehovah God!

In closing, please note this: To sign-up with God means to allow Him to have dominion of your ambitions, desires, plans, and goals. Does He have dominion of your life? Have you signed up with God yet?

Neh'enah.

35

Setting Order in Your Spirit, Soul, and Body!

"Only take heed to yourself, and diligently keep yourself, lest you forget the things your eyes have seen, and lest they depart from your heart all the days of your life." (Deuteronomy 4:9)

In meditating upon the words of Moses, the servant of the Lord, I came upon this portion about being **"diligent to keep yourself."**

I believe that the first and most powerful revelation given to man is coming to the knowledge of Christ.

To be born-again has to be the ultimate experience ever granted to mankind. Imagine the Creator of the universe coming into you and living inside your heart? Wow!

When Christ comes into your heart, your whole being is awakened to the reality of why you were created. Your spirit-man becomes your Guide, and the beginning of an endless life in God begins!

The second greatest revelation that I have discovered in my own life is the revelation of personal development.

Personal development in my mind, has to do with taking responsibility for the vessel that God has graciously created.

Indeed, God has given us a body with a soul and spirit. But, in addition to that we have been created intelligently and, we have a purpose to fulfill here on earth.

It's Not a Bad Thing!

I have heard many believers reject the teachings of personal development, claiming that God has everything under control, and that He knows what to do with every circumstance. Therefore, there is absolutely no need to seek any type of personal development of any kind.

They believe that personal development is a new age thing— a tool for self-aggrandizing— or some curriculum to develop a humanistic mindset.

I totally disagree.

Let me just say that personal development can be a trap for anything ungodly to come into our lives,(if we leave Christ out of the equation).

If we do it for ourselves, then yes, we would be missing the point. Jesus must be the center of everything!

Learning in the light of eternity for the glory of God and the expansion of His kingdom is one thing, but learning for the sole purpose of accomplishing some great feat for selfish gain, would be more about expanding the kingdom of self. We have the opportunity to choose.

What About the Vessel God Made?

Developing your God-given life is just as important as breathing!

Unless you are willing to remain ignorant for the rest of your life, one must better get to seeking all they can about becoming that vessel God designed.

There are many areas and subjects we must learn about such as: finances, relationships, work ethics, health, the deeper spiritual life, administration, and countless other subjects that will make us better prepared for greater impact
.

The kingdom of God is about advancing the cause of Christ upon the earth. It's about being a light in a dark corner; a testimony of a new nature— a manifestation of God's glory upon the earth.

God begins the work deep within our spirit— after that, our life becomes awakened to the countless possibilities that we can have, if we listen to God's voice.

Brokenness Is a Must!

Unless a man or woman understands brokenness, he or she will be led astray by their own will or desires. Their own hearts will deceive them!

A person must truly realize that Jesus Christ must have the preeminence in all things before one can study personal development.

To fully appreciate the value of personal development, one must see it [personal development,] from God's perspective first.

Understanding that God is and must be first in all things all the time, is, the beginning of great wisdom.

Everything that surrounds us, everything we think and do, all of it, has been granted to us for Him alone. It's all about Jesus!

Let me close with these words…

Trust in the Lord with all your heart, and lean not on your own understanding; In all your ways acknowledge Him; and He shall direct your paths." (Proverbs 3:5,6)

Neh'enah.

36

The Accommodation for the Revelation!

"At that time the Lord said to me, 'Hew for yourself two tablets of stone like the first, and come up to Me on the mountain and make yourself an ark of wood. And I will write on the tablets the words that were on the first tablets, which you broke; and you shall put them in the ark.' So, I made an ark of acacia wood, hewed two tablets of stone like the first, and went up the mountain, having the two tablets in my hand. And He wrote on the tablets according to the first writing, the Ten Commandments, which the Lord had spoken to you in the mountain from the midst of the fire in the day of the assembly; and the Lord gave them to me. Then I turned and came down from the mountain and put the tablets in the ark which I had made; and there they are, just as the Lord commanded me." (Deuteronomy 10:1-5)

During my quiet time today, my spirit was caught up in God's revelation of getting things done on earth.

Whatever is important to the Lord, He will communicate it to His servants. It's up to the servant to hear God's desire and make himself available to follow through with God's wish.

Such was the case with the second set of stone tablets where the Lord wrote out the Ten Commandments.

It Starts with a Relationship

In a close relationship, we tend to be more intune with detail.

If you are close to someone and get along with them, you will allow yourself to be influenced by them.

Now, if you love someone, not only will you be influenced by them, but you will want to know more details about them: their likes and dislikes, things that move them emotionally, and things that don't; every preference is closely monitored, all because of proximity.

It is the same way with God.

As we allow ourselves to be touched by God, we will experience His very heart in all things. We will desire what He desires; we will hate what He hates; we will do things that please Him and bring Him pleasure.

In Tune with God

After the first set of tablets with the Ten Commandments had been destroyed due to the wrath of Moses in response to the idolatry from God's children, the Lord told Moses to **"hew [cut into shape] for himself a new set of stone tables, like the first."**

Also, the Lord told Moses to make an ark of acacia wood, to put the tablets in it.

Notice: The revelation fromGod was the Ten Commandments. This was God's part. The "hewing" of the tablets of stone and the making of an ark of acacia wood, was Moses' part.

The new tablets of stone and the rewriting of the Ten Commandments was contingent upon the obedience of Moses. If Moses said, "I'm not 'hewing' anything!"

Who knows how this story might have ended?

What If...

"And I will write on the tablets the words that were on the first tablets, which you broke; and you shall put them in the ark.'"

I started thinking about this as I meditated: What if Moses said, "No God! I'm not doing this!" What do you suppose the Lord would have done?

You see, God will first share the intent, the vision, the plan with us. Then, He will move accordingly.

If you make preparations for the revelation, He will honor all that you do to accommodate it.

We must learn to live this way.

I have heard it said time and time again: "God does the supernatural, and we do the natural!"

I believe this. God will first download the idea, then we need to accommodate it by providing the hands and feet.

We must ask God to make us more sensible to this philosophy of living.

He leads with a roar; we follow with a submissive spirit.

Whatever He needs for us to do to make His dream come true – in this, we should occupy ourselves. This is what it truly means to be about the Father's business! Neh'enah.

37

What Can Two Coins Buy Me?

"Looking up, [Jesus] saw the rich people putting their gifts into the treasury. And He saw also a poor widow putting in two mites (copper coins). And He said, Truly I say to you, this poor widow has put in more than all of them; For they all gave out of their abundance (their surplus); but she has contributed out of her lack and her want, putting in all that she had on which to live." (Luke 21:1-4)

Here's an interesting story I found as I meditated upon God's Word in regard to laying it all out without reserves, regrets, or retreats.

This is the story of a poor widow who Jesus happened to keep His eye on as the time for giving offerings at the temple took place.

The first thing that Jesus noticed was how the rich were putting their gifts into the treasury and at the same time, a poor widow showed up with her offering.

So, something out of the ordinary happened, to everyone's surprise if I may add, Jesus commended the widow for her offering. He said, **"Truly I say to you, this poor widow has put in more than all of them!"**
Can you imagine everyone thinking and in essence saying, "Jesus, come on! Didn't you see the amount the rich put in? That poor widow does not even come close to the offering what the rich gave!"

Giving Out of Our Surplus

To everyone's amazement, Jesus said, **"For they [the rich] all gave out of their abundance (their surplus); but she has contributed out of her lack and her want, putting in all that she had on which to live."**

In the economy of God, it is really all about the heart.

Jesus was not impressed by the amount given by the rich, not because it wasn't a good amount, but rather, He was moved because their hearts were reserved to give abundantly!

Put It in Jesus' Wallet!

On the other hand, the widow, **"...contributed out of her lack and her want, putting it all that she had on which to live."**

In other words, Jesus noticed that this woman really had nothing to cling onto, but God. What good were two coins in her possession, versus putting those two coins in the hands of God?
The spiritual man will always have a deeper reason for laying his life down.

Risk-taking is truly an easy thing to do when you catch a glimpse of where you are headed!

There is no doubt in my mind that this woman lived her life with eternal values in view.

If we were to ask the widow, "Why did you risk giving everything you had?"

She would probably reply something like this: "Seriously, do you think two pennies are going to get me a better life?"

She understood that true joy was in giving not in getting!

She would probably blow our minds away and say, *"I gave it all because for two coins, I get to have free breath, free life, free sunshine, a view of the sunset, as well as a great opportunity to tell God that He is my everything!"*

Let us learn to give until it hurts— until we can't give anymore. Yes, until the Lord knows that we are more in love with Him than anything else!

Neh'enah.

38

When You Go Out to Battle!

"When you go out to battle against your enemies and see horses and chariots and people more numerous than you, do not be afraid of them; for the Lord your God is with you, who brought you up from the land of Egypt." (Deuteronomy 20:1)

One of the most powerful human tendencies has to be the temptation to fall into fear. How often in life have we faced strong opposition or contrary winds?

I bet the experiences are too many to count. Everyone will be challenged in due time, but those who overcome will inherit the promises!

The Face of Fear

In pondering this particular Scripture, I was reminded of a dear friend of mine who had come to the place of being challenged by a particular sickness. By God's healing power he is alive today, but I also know that many don't survive their sicknesses.

It has been my experience as a minister of the gospel to see people totally fall apart when they hear the word cancer. Let me say that these doctors' reports can be extremely scary and very paralyzing. Please understand that I'm in no way making light of any sickness.

Oftentimes I get phone calls from people who will share out of a broken heart, "Pastor David, the doctor said the lab work is in and they found cancer!" This is usually followed by a long silence and an endless pool of tears.

It is Not Easy to Rise!

When challenged with uncertainty, when faced with a deadly sickness or a life-taking obstacle, we are challenged by the Lord to not be afraid of them. To this I have too many times said, Easier said than done! How many are with me?

But why did the Lord say this regarding His children in a time of battle? Jehovah God understood that His children had nothing to cling to but Him! The Lord knew that if His children didn't follow His counsel, they would be drowning in fear and overcome by it.

So, here is what the Lord laid out as instruction to overcome an enemy more numerous than they…

A Solid Reference

"When you go out to battle against your enemies and see horses and chariots and people more numerous than you, do not be afraid of them; for the Lord your God is with you, who brought you up from the land of Egypt."

Quickly the Lord makes reference to a couple of things:

1. **"More numerous than you..."** – this speaks of overcoming something that has you outnumbered in emotions, outnumbered in faith, outnumbered physically, outnumbered in knowledge, etc.

2. **"do not be afraid..."** – this type of fear leads to panic. So, God says, "Don't do it!" Once we panic, we can't think straight.

3. **"...for the Lord God is with you..."** – by faith, we appropriate this one fact: God is with us! You only have to believe it, so that the download of Himself can come down to you. The Scripture says, "Greater is He that is in you than he that is in the world." (1 John 4:4)

4. **"...who brought you up from the land of Egypt."** – encourages us to remember the history of God's powerful defeat over the Egyptians. Through signs and wonders, God gave His children the victory! It would be wise for any servant of God to ponder the great testimonies of God's delivering power over and over again!

In closing, I believe that fear is a weapon of the enemy. Yet, I also believe that we are called to walk by faith and not by sight. Walking by sight is a trap to God's advancement, while faith is the highway to all His promises!

Neh'enah.

39

Who is Taking You Up to the Mountain?

"Then the devil, taking Him up on a high mountain, showed Him all the kingdoms of the world in a moment of time. And the devil said to Him, 'All this authority I will give You, and their glory; for this has been delivered to me, and I give it to whomever I wish. Therefore, if You will worship before me, all will be Yours.'

And Jesus answered and said to him, 'Get behind Me, Satan! For it is written, "You shall worship the Lord your God, and Him only you shall serve."'" (Luke 4:5-8)

It would probably be a fair comment and say that most people are ambitious for something greater in life.

Many people have desires to achieve great goals and express themselves to the uttermost extent with their ideas and philosophies.

The temptation then would be to outdo oneself. This temptation is ever present and the real challenge to all this is to stay put in your present sphere until your name is called to another sphere.

My spiritual mentor used to always say to me, "David, anyone can convince themselves that they bought a good used car." In other words, anyone can convince themselves that they are right and the whole world is wrong!

What is a Sphere?

For starters, what is a sphere? The word sphere in Merriam-Webster's dictionary means *an area or range over or within which someone or something acts, exists, or has influence or significance.*

We are all placed in a sphere and in this sphere, we move and have our being. We abide in it, develop in it and express ourselves in it.

For the people of God, the people of faith, God has established a sphere for His children. We abide in it, for it is God who has placed us there. So, we want to be obedient and stay within our boundaries.

When the Test Comes!

If you will notice an interesting thing in the Scripture I am using – Jesus is taken up on a high mountain –yes, to another sphere.

In that sphere, the devil shows Him all the kingdoms of the world. He proceeds to tell Jesus that all of these kingdoms are his and he can give them to whomever he wishes....wow!

The temptation here is for Jesus to move into another sphere before His time – one that God had not given him yet.

This is a test for all of humanity. You and I will be tested in the area of spheres. We will be seduced to move into something that God has never intended for us to have, or at least not have at that particular moment in time.

The devil presented a plan to Jesus and in essence said, **"I will give you what your eyes have caught a glimpse of. I will let you experience all this glory, if only you will bow and worship before me."**

It Is Through Our Eyes!

It is through our eyes that we become trapped in a sphere that is not ours. Our hearts will deceive us; we will then start saying to ourselves: "God wants me to have it all!"

A Word of Caution

Let me just say something from my heart to yours: "Don't ever become seduced by the enemy when he presents a sphere that looks tantalizing. If it feels good to the flesh, it probably is not God. If you have to have it now, it is probably not God speaking to you.

"Be wise as a serpent, but gentle as a dove" in all your dealings. Know that your time will come – for the Lord Himself will go before you and establish you!

Neh'enah.

40

Yesterday's Success, Tomorrow's Promises, and the God-Effect!

> **"Blessed be the name of God forever and ever,**
> **For wisdom and might are His.**
> **And He changes the times and the seasons; He re moves kings and raises up kings;**
> **He gives wisdom to the wise**
> **And knowledge to those who have understanding."** (Daniel 2:20-21)

A few days back I had been meditating about the seasons of the Lord in my life and how all the different seasons in our lives serve a purpose.

Also, I pondered on how the Lord is "Lord of all," but has delegated unto us His children, the power to make choices, and therefore the ability to make changes.

The Lord has given us the will to choose. We can choose to do right or to do wrong at any time or at any place; yet in all this, every decision will carry its own consequence.

The reaping effect to our decisions will be based upon our sowing and so forth.

Is It Time to Let Go?

To this I want to say that oftentimes, we fall into a trap of holding on to last season's blessing or at least in our estimation, we see it as a blessing.

Though something was really good last season, it will more than likely not be as good in your present season.

Let me illustrate:

I have fruit trees in the backyard of my ministry base offices. These trees produce some of the most wonderful oranges this country will ever know – (I'm exaggerating, but just a bit)!

Some of these oranges never get taken down so they hang on the branch till the following season, believe it or not.

Obviously, once orange has been ripe for a long time – it is probably not edible by the next season.

Without any consciousness, the fruit doesn't know that it is probably not good to the taste anymore, but it insists on holding on.

This reminds me of our human nature. We hold on to things produced from last season to the point where we fight for the right to keep it!

We have a hard time letting go of yesterday's successes and truly block or dam-up the new fruit coming forth.

At first, we don't see this. We are adamant about keeping everything the way it has been and vow to keep it that way! We have all done it.

Welcome to the God-Effect!

In all this, there is a God-effect!

Even if we are not willing to let the fruit of yesterday go, the Lord Himself will change the seasons.

If the old fruit must go, and we are unwilling to let it go, God Himself will change the season and dry it all up until it falls to the ground – for the season has changed and it is time you realized it!

I believe many of the traditions we hold onto in life have this as a basis.

Fear paralyzes!

Most of the time, we don't make changes due to fear. It is not the only reason, but to me, it is one of the most paralyzing of all emotions.

Let me close by just saying that when the season to reap is here, it is hard to sow— and when the time to sow has come, it is hard for anyone to reap.

It would be wise for us to lend ourselves to the wisdom of understanding the season of life we are in with God.

To know if we should let go or not is a major key component to future fruitfulness.

Neh'enah.

41

Face to Face Leadership!

"But since then there has not arisen in Israel a prophet like Moses, whom the Lord knew face to face, in all the signs and wonders which the Lord sent him to do in the land of Egypt, before Pharaoh, before all his servants, and in all his land, and by all that mighty power and all the great terror which Moses performed in the sight of all Israel." (Deuteronomy 34:10-12)

The Scripture above states that **"...there has not arisen in Israel a prophet like Moses, whom the Lord knew face to face."**

Obviously, the Lord and Moses had a very unique relationship dating back to his birth not to mention the immeasurable favor God had afforded him while under the leadership of Pharaoh.

By reading about the life of Moses, one could make the argument that Moses was living the life! That Moses had it made in the shade. Everything was at his disposal: authority, favor, splendor, and status. Moses was without a doubt, a great asset to the Pharaoh.

Created for So Much More!

Yet in the life of Moses, or should I say, inside the heart of Moses, something else was dying to come out – the reason why he was created, his purpose, if you will.

There was no way of Pharaoh knowing about these emotions inside of Moses. There was nothing no one could do to pacify the longings and desires inside the heart of Moses.

I can only imagine him [Moses] living day by day and coming home completely consumed by feelings of dissatisfaction and tension. Have you ever felt this in your own heart? I have.

Worldly Leadership

Moses was awakened to greatness, even as a young boy. He was taken-in early to the most educated places and was taught skills and was perhaps mentored by the very best the world system could offer.

All this was well and good until he reached the inevitable — the place where no man could go, the place reserved by God for God - his eternal purpose!

Listen to this: **"By faith Moses, when he became of age, refused to be called the son of Pharaoh's daughter, choosing rather to suffer affliction with the people of God than to enjoy the passing pleasures of sin, esteeming the reproach of Christ greater riches than the treasures in Egypt; for he looked to the reward. By faith he forsook Egypt, not fearing the wrath of the king; for he endured as seeing Him who is invisible."** (Hebrews 11:24-27)

When you and I reach a certain age, (this is not a number, but rather a place of receptivity where the purpose of God becomes more tangible we will not want the riches of Egypt anymore.

These things will no longer enslave us and have a hold on us; they will not drive us like some harsh taskmaster!

Fine-Tuning the Sound of His Voice

Don't get me wrong, we will still have all the leadership zest we have always had, but the purpose of why we were created will take a different form.

Our hearts will capture a different sound of Who it is that is leading us; yes, it will be the voice of the One who created us, our Commander in Chief.

For us to be led by God, we will need to learn to stay put and wait for His call. The longings of our hearts will dictate our next move.

Face to face leadership is all about hearing His word, reading His facial expressions and moving by the beat of His emotions.

To have face to face encounters with God will be the norm, as we must pursue the purpose of why we were created.

Let me close by saying that only face to face leadership will get us to the place of God's original intent, original design, and pleasure!

Neh'enah.

42

No Holy Spirit Means No Power!

"Some fell on rock; and as soon as it sprang up, it withered away because it lacked moisture." (Luke 8:6)

This morning I came outside to my backyard to do some praying and some writing, and while I conversed with God, I felt the Lord showing me one more time, it is not the fancy footwork of a minister's skills and theatrics that changes the human heart.

It still amazes me how many Christian leaders and churches continue to make the effort in trying to bring about life transformations without the power of God, without the Spirit of God!

In reading the verses about the **"sower who went out to sow,"** I was reminded of this topic.

Why Am I Disturbed?

I so appreciate all the efforts from ministers all over America— the television and radio broadcastings, the videos, the propaganda to advance the kingdom of God.

Yet in all this, the sense I get from Christians is that they are having shallow encounters with religion and not actually the King of Kings! They are coming in contact with a religious program but not a face to face encounter with Jesus the Lord! This has me disturbed.

While I meditated upon this particular verse of Luke 8:6, the Holy Spirit took me to this one particular word, moisture.

It says or gives the understanding that the [seed] sprang up, and then it withered away! Why? It lacked moisture according to the wise words of Jesus.

Let's go a little deeper here:

Lack of Moisture means no water in the dirt. Water is a type and symbol of the Holy Spirit! There is no mistaking the message of Jesus here – if there is no water then no life can come to the seed!

Much of what I see in the ministry today, is nothing more than good theology, good Bible studies and sermons, great rhythmic songs and poetry, great lights and theatrics, and in some places, delicious coffee – yet through all of these endeavors, there is nothing in this recipe that produces life! None whatsoever!

Content with Nothing!

People are content to keep meeting service after service, bible study after bible study, discipleship session after discipleship session, praise and worship songs after praise and worship songs, with no life-changing experiences with God.

Ministers are content to stand in pulpits today without

one drop of water to produce moisture for the incubation and/or germinating of new life to come forth. It has all become too standard, a one-size fits all Christianity.

Personal Prayer Brings the Moisture

You and I have nothing but dirt to work with. It is until the Holy Spirit flows through us that moisture builds. As we deliver God's revelation of His Word, then His life begins to flourish and then springs forth His expression.

As we go forth in Jesus' Name – let us be filled with the Holy Spirit who is the power of God! Then and only then, can we see a life transformed and empowered to carry out God's wishes on the earth.

Neh'enah.

43

Seeing the Invisible!

"While He was still speaking, someone came from the ruler of the synagogue's house, saying to him, 'Your daughter is dead. Do not trouble the Teacher.' But when Jesus heard it, He answered him, saying, 'Do not be afraid; only believe, and she will be made well.' When He came into the house, He permitted no one to go in except Peter, James, and John, and the father and mother of the girl. Now all wept and mourned for her; but He said, 'Do not weep; she is not dead, but sleeping.' And they ridiculed Him, knowing that she was dead. But He put them all outside, took her by the hand and called, saying, 'Little girl, arise.' Then her spirit returned, and she arose immediately. And He commanded that she be given something to eat. And her parents were astonished, but He charged them to tell no one what had happened."
(Luke 8:49-56)

People who have lived by faith and have walked by faith in times past, always seem to have become the mockery of their day.

During the great healing revivals of the 1950's, people would actually be healed instantly under tent meetings because they had faith. They had the faith of God!

It is amazing to see how people who walk in the real faith of God operate.

Why Are You Different?

Everything they do is different in comparison to the people that normally surround them. For example: They think differently, they talk different, and they act different.

Oftentimes, the way they move and process life – is also very different.

Is it any wonder why people would literally ridicule Jesus? It is not the Lord's fault for His ability to see the spiritual realm!

In the Scripture that I have shared with you on this devotion, Jesus is called on to go and pray for a sick girl who was believed to be recently deceased.

To this, after Jesus heard that the little girl had died, commented, **"Do not weep; she is not dead, but sleeping."**

To this one comment, those who heard him say this, ridiculed him. They made fun of Jesus for seeing death as equivalent to sleeping. Amazing!

People who walk in the realm of the Spirit, have this ability to see death as an equivalent to sleeping. They see impossibilities as possible things! They see things that are not as if they already were! Jesus saw this little girl who had just died as just taking a nap!

Eyes to See How Things Really Are!

After dealing with those mockers, (by putting them outside of the house) the Scripture says, He proceeded to take care of business: **"But He put them all outside, took her by the hand and called, saying, 'Little girl, arise.' Then her spirit returned, and she arose immediately."**

What is interesting to me in these verses is the contrast of thought.

Those who heard of the young lady dying, saw it as the end of a life; Jesus saw it as an opportunity to demonstrate God's mighty power over death.

The mockers saw it as an impossibility; Jesus saw the little girl's life from heaven's perspective as it really was.

The next time you are challenged by natural circumstances, keep in mind with what eyes are you seeing it? Are you seeing with your natural eyes or with your spiritual eyes? Your perception will manifest your results!

Neh'enah.

44

Our Challenge is Bigger than Giants!

"Therefore take careful heed to yourselves, that you love the Lord your God. Or else, if indeed you do go back, and cling to the remnant of these nations—these that remain among you—and make marriages with them, and go into them and they to you, know for certain that the Lord your God will no longer drive out these nations from before you. But they shall be snares and traps to you, and scourges on your sides and thorns in your eyes, until you perish from this good land which the Lord your God has given you." (Joshua 23:11-13)

It is my belief that the love for Jesus will always be our safeguard as we venture along life's path.

The challenge will not be the giants we encounter in life — the challenge for every spirit-filled believer will always be keeping the fire of God's love burning bright within!

I was thinking as I meditated upon these verses this past weekend, how in comparison to other nations, Israel was unique in every way.

In their natural strength, they were not more powerful than other nations; they were actually weaker. Yet, it pleased God to select the Israelites as his chosen people. There is no doubt in my mind that what made Israel powerful, was God's favor upon them!

God's Favor Makes the Difference

If God is pleased with us, I believe that there is nothing God will not do for us.

The Lord established some awesome promises for His people if they would be willing to follow His lead.

I believe it is the same with us. The examples that God laid out for us are clearly seen on these verses. Listen to this: **"...if indeed you do go back, and cling to the remnant of these nations—these that remain among you—and make marriages with them, and go in to them and they to you, know for certain that the Lord your God will no longer drive out these nations from before you."**

Here is what I get: If our love wanes for Jesus, it leaves a door open for another to come in and take God's place in our hearts.

Clinging to something by force means that God will not fight on our behalf. He will just turn us over to what our heart really wants —to be married to another and not Him!

The Outcome!

After the Lord turns away, the enemy will have his way with us. We will be scourged by the enemy! This means that our destiny will probably not be what God intended.

It will be nothing but pain and struggle until we perish from the good land that the Lord had given us.

Before we follow the desires of our own heart, we should consult with the Holy Spirit first. Let us make sure that we are following the desires in God's heart.

Neh'enah

45

Are You Worried and Troubled A bout Many Things?

"Now it happened as they went that He entered a certain village; and a certain woman named Martha welcomed Him into her house. And she had a sister called Mary, who also sat at Jesus' feet and heard His word. But Martha was distracted with much serving, and she approached Him and said, 'Lord, do You not care that my sister has left me to serve alone? Therefore tell her to help me.' And Jesus answered and said to her, 'Martha, Martha, you are worried and troubled about many things. But one thing is needed, and Mary has chosen that good part, which will not be taken away from her.'" (Luke 10:38-42)

I can't tell you how many times I have read this one particular passage and it never fails, that God's Spirit, always quickens my heart and mind with it.

In previous studies and meditations of the verses above, I have looked deeply into the life of Martha, the life of Mary and the whole situation at their house; all I have to say is that these were two different people (though related as sisters) with obvious aspirations to please God.

Sitting at the Feet of Jesus

First of all, we have Mary.

Mary had developed a custom or a certain practice anytime Jesus was around. She would sit at his feet and open her heart to hear the wisdom and understanding of God.

She could have been running around in the kitchen making supper, but no – she chose to sit at the feet of the Master.

Let me just say that serving God is not a bad thing whatsoever – as a matter of fact, it is exactly the thing to do when you have a relationship with God.

Secondly, we have the other sister by the name of Martha.

Apparently, the gift of hospitality was very strong in her life and there is no doubt about that.

She welcomed Jesus into the house, she headed towards the kitchen to make Him something to eat, but she also complained when she received no help from her sister Mary.

Can You Serve to a Fault?

As I said earlier, serving is not a bad thing at all. Unless, serving becomes your distraction, then you might want to revisit and evaluate your life once again.
Here's what Jesus gave as wisdom for all who would want to be His servants: **"But Martha was distracted with much serving, and she approached Him and said, 'Lord, do You not care that my sister has left me to serve alone? Therefore tell her to help me.' And Jesus answered and said to her, 'Martha, Martha, you are worried and trou-**

bled about many things. But one thing is needed, and Mary has chosen that good part, which will not be taken away from her.'"

The Scripture points out one major characteristic in the life of Martha. It says she was **"distracted with much serving."**

Many might see this as a plus, but the Scripture makes it sound a bit more like a deficiency. Let us look at it deeper...

The word *distracted* means to be or become distracted; conceived of as if pulling someone away.

Have You Felt the Pull?

Let me ask you a question: Have you ever felt like you were being pulled away from something valuable? Pulled away from something critical? Have you? What is pulling you, do you know? Have you been honest enough to admit what it is that is pulling you away?

Martha without even knowing it, she was being pulled away from hearing and learning the heart of God. She was **"...worried and troubled about many things."**

Just like Martha, there are many servants of the Lord who allow themselves to fall into this category of going all out to serve God simply because they are not complete in Him.

I don't know what it was in Martha's life that was pulling her away from what was truly valuable, but something was!

I'm not saying that Martha was trying to cover up a deeper issue but apparently, she was being motivated by something or someone to act this way.

I have met some "Marthas" in my life. Here is what I have learned from them: They feel the need to serve to please rather than the need to sit and worship.

Before we act, one must understand who it is that stands before them.

How many more times would Jesus visit these two sisters? Who knows, but Mary was not taking any chances. She was going to take the time to sit and take notes of what exactly God was thinking, saying, and doing at the time!

As I close this devotion, remember not to get distracted by anything. Jesus must always be our priority in all things.

Neh'enah.

46

Mighty through God!

"Then the Lord turned to him and said, 'Go in this might of yours, and you shall save Israel from the hand of the Midianites. Have I not sent you?' So he said to Him, O my Lord, how can I save Israel? Indeed my clan is the weakest in Manasseh, and I am the least in my father's house.' And the Lord said to him, 'Surely I will be with you, and you shall defeat the Midianites as one man.'" (Judges 6:14-16)

Meditating upon Gideon's experience with God, I came to a sobering reality on this day. I came to the realization that God only needs cooperation from His servants, nothing else.

The supernatural enduement of power comes from God, but the vessel (though made out of clay) is still the instrument God has chosen to work through.

I want to bring forth some interesting points out of these verses and prayerfully take you into a deeper revelation of God's intent.

In this Might of Yours!

Here we find a simple but also intriguing perspective of how God thinks. The Scripture says that the Lord told Gideon to, **"Go in this might of yours, and you shall save Israel..."**

What exactly does this mean? I believe that this means cooperation.

All God wanted and literally needed from Gideon was for him to move in obedience. This included for Gideon to embrace God's thoughts, emotions, and vision.

To all this, the Lord follows it up with an affirming statement: **"Have I not sent you?"**

These words made all the difference in the world! Without this affirmation coming from the Lord, there is no way on earth that Gideon would have the guts to do what he did in defeating the Midianites.

How Can I Save Israel?

After the Lord had affirmed Gideon, something in this servant still did not activate. What was it? The thing that did not activate in Gideon was that Gideon was full of himself.

He still kept looking at his own condition and status. He still saw himself as helpless, weak, and useless.

Do you think God knew all this? Of course He did!
I believe that this is one of the main reasons God chose Gideon.

He needed someone who understood their real condition— a condition of helplessness and poverty. Only this way, God would get all the glory after the battle would be won.

I believe this is one of the reasons God chooses people who are humble and broken; He knows that they are so ready to embrace His love and power!

The Least in My Father's House

"...and I am the least in my father's house." Gideon truly had no confidence in himself and to trust God was a real challenge for him.

Gideon said that he was "the least" in his father's house. This probably meant that he was pretty much nothing to no one— a bona fide "nobody." Yet it pleased God to use him just as he was — fearful and all!

We are So Much Like Gideon!

I truly believe that you and I are just like Gideon in so many ways. He is the epitome of the human vessel who felt worthless and useless until God intervened in some supernatural way.

In closing, I want us to note this one thing: God needs our cooperation. He will instill in us all He needs us to know, and all He needs us to do!

All we need to do is position ourselves to hear His words and then obey them!

Neh'enah.

47

COVID-19, Uncertainty and the Will of God!

"Therefore whoever hears these sayings of Mine, and does them, I will liken him to a wise man who built his house on the rock: and the rain descended, the floods came, and the winds blew and beat on that house; and it did not fall, for it was founded on the rock. But everyone who hears these sayings of Mine, and does not do them, will be like a foolish man who built his house on the sand: and the rain descended, the floods came, and the winds blew and beat on that house; and it fell. And great was its fall." (Matthew 7:24-27)

Not to make light of any adverse situation, but much of what affects our lives has to do with our perception of how we see things from the place where we stand.

Obviously, if you are making the attempt to get out of a

vast forest without a roadmap, you might find it very difficult.

Now, if you are flying on a plane, you will be able to get a better view of where you are, and therefore decide which road to take in the midst of that forest.

In Times of Uncertainty

During difficult and adverse times, it is easy to look outside of ourselves and start looking at our surroundings and start blaming people, situations, and other external means for our demise. This happens all the time.

As we have been facing a pandemic in our nation, many feel that they didn't ask for this situation in their lives.

They feel that they need to blame someone for what has taken place these last few months, yet, that is a choice we all make. Should we blame someone for what they are facing personally or corporately? Let us look further…

Storms Hit Everyone!

When Jesus speaks of the man who built his house on the rock and the other man who built his house on sand, he is literally speaking about making choices.

Taking into account what happened to these two builders, one can see that it is not about the storm coming. Storms hit us all. We all have them in our lives!

Where you might be standing during the storm, is perhaps the rightful and more precise question to ask here.

Obviously, one builder built on sand. Everyone knows that sand is not a solid ground or foundation to build upon! Yet, many have gone on to build their ideas, philosophies, and their dreams upon sand. When the storm comes up, the man-made dream comes tumbling down.

Are times hard for everyone? I say they are very challenging for all. How will things end up when it is all said and done? Well, that totally depends on where you are standing!

If you are standing upon the rock, you will not be moved.

If you are standing on a foundation of sand, I'm afraid that your most valuable commodities such as time, money, and emotions —will all go to waste!

Neh'enah.

48

Learn to Finish Well!

"Then the Philistines took him and put out his eyes and brought him down to Gaza. They bound him with bronze fetters, and he became a grinder in the prison." (Judges 16:21)

Contemplating on the life story of Samson today, I came to a place of understanding a whole lot more about what was at stake for this servant of God.

Samson was born out of barrenness, and the Lord had charged Samson's parents to keep a Nazirite vow on him for life.

This was a tall order for anyone to keep, yet God needed this kind of man for the kind of work that awaited him.

If you have read all the story of Samson or at least part of it, you will quickly notice that this was no ordinary man.

Samson was a man with the touch of God. God had called him out and Samson was determined to follow God at all cost.

In all his pursuits of God, Samson was also very human. He had issues with impatience, issues with strange women, and wanted the best of both worlds.
I am not sure how long one can get away with this lifestyle, but surely it would soon catch up with Samson.

The Philistines hated Samson and they were consumed with the idea of shutting him down. At any cost, the Philistines would pursue this powerful man of God!

Up to this point in history, Samson had gotten away with a reckless lifestyle, and with an irresponsible approach to the seriousness of God, Samson would eventually be his own greatest enemy.

Delilah was the Tool

The Scriptures say, "**Afterward it happened that he loved a woman in the Valley of Sorek, whose name was Delilah.**" (Judges 16:4)

The great controversy at the center of Samson's life was that he "loved" a woman in the Valley of Sorek! The word "loved," means to have great affection or care or loyalty towards.

Little did Samson know what was about to come his way. He should have known that the end to all this would end up in shame and despair and blindness!

Is it Possible to be that Careless?

Samson shared his whole heart with Delilah and revealed the secret of his great strength to the "devil" himself.

Once the truth of his strength was revealed, it would be

just a matter of time before the enemy would divide and conquer this man of God!

After Samson shared his whole heart with Delilah, the Philistines came and took him.

Samson felt confident that he could break the ropes, but he didn't know that this one time, the Lord was no longer working with him. Can you imagine this?

What did Samson lose? He lost his name, his freedom, and his eyes!

What Is Life without God's Vision?

As I close this meditation, I want to reflect a bit on the pain of not being able to see.

To not be able to see God, not be able to see what God is doing, and to not have the freedom to do all that is in the heart of God has to be one of the hardest and saddest chapters in anyone's life!

The cry of God here is: Start by faith and finish well! We must learn to finish well!
Neh'enah.

49

Please Have Me Excused!

"Now when one of those who sat at the table with Him heard these things, he said to Him, 'Blessed is he who shall eat bread in the kingdom of God!' Then He said to him, 'A certain man gave a great supper and invited many, and sent his servant at supper time to say to those who were invited, Come, for all things are now ready.' But they all with one accord began to make excuses. The first said to him, 'I have bought a piece of ground, and I must go and see it. I ask you to have me excused.' And another said, 'I have bought five yoke of oxen, and I am going to test them. I ask you to have me excused.' Still another said, 'I have married a wife, and therefore I cannot come.' So that servant came and reported these things to his master. Then the master of the house, being angry, said to his servant, 'Go out quickly into the streets and lanes of the city, and bring in here the poor and the

maimed and the lame and the blind.'" (Luke 14:15-21)

When it comes to following the Lord, and I mean following with the heart, not being "wishy-washy" and negligent with His will and His call, one will be placed on probation by the Holy Spirit on a daily basis.

The Spirit of the Lord will guide you into all truth and will take you to places deep within your spirit to evaluate your heart.

We usually know what things own us or control us by how we defend them or make excuses for them.

In the passage above, Jesus points out the fact that when it comes to the kingdom of God and partaking of it, people tend to be quick to give excuses about why they can't participate.

First of all, we have the man who made the first excuse. He said, "'I have bought a piece of ground, and I must go and see it."

His first excuse dealt with his personal space. When the Lord begins to deal with you – it comes with the intent to invade your personal space. He wants in on all of you, not just part of you.

The second man who was invited to the banquet said this for an excuse, "I have bought five yoke of oxen, and I am going to test them."

The second evaluation will deal with your personal possessions.

Do you love your toys more than Jesus? Tough one! Are you ready to relinquish your rights and turn them over to God? Allow Him to be the One who sets in order your possessions. Trust me, He will ask you to give up your rights over them.

The third man who was invited also, made an excuse. His

excuse was the following, **"I have married a wife, and therefore I cannot come."**

This evaluation deals with your heart. Is your heart all for God? Is He holding first place in your life? Are there things that have your heart's control?

Whatever the case may be – if you long to grow in the Lord and move on to greater places in God, it will cost you something.

If an experience of God doesn't cost you anything, it will do nothing!

Neh'enah.

50

Kissing Your Future Goodbye!

"And Naomi said to her two daughters-in-law, 'Go, return each to her mother's house. The Lord deal kindly with you, as you have dealt with the dead and with me. The Lord grants that you may find rest, each in the house of her husband.' So she kissed them, and they lifted up their voices and wept. And they said to her, 'Surely we will return with you to your people.' But Naomi said, 'Turn back, my daughters; why will you go with me? Are there still sons in my womb, that they may be your husbands? Turn back, my daughters, go—for I am too old to have a husband. If I should say I have hope, if I should have a husband tonight and should also bear sons, would you wait for them till they were grown? Would you restrain yourselves from having husbands? No, my daughters; for it grieves me very much for your sakes that the hand of the Lord has gone out against me!'

Then they lifted up their voices and wept again; and Orpah kissed her mother-in-law, but Ruth clung to her." (Ruth 1:8-14)

Knowing when to say goodbye to a situation is not as easy as it sounds.

Too many times we let go too early, and then realize later on how we should have held on a bit longer.
I admit, some of these lessons are hard to learn, but nevertheless, they have to be learned if we are ever going to enter in our destiny, or at least in the flow of having a greater opportunity for a better future.

In the story above [Read Ruth 1:1-7] we discover that Elimelech and Naomi had two children, Mahlon and Chilion. This family came from Bethlehem, Judah and moved to Moab, for there was a famine back in Judah. Mahlon and Chilion both married and lived in Moab.

The day came when their father Elimelech died and so did

they. The only survivors now were Naomi, and her two daughters-in-law, Ruth and Orpah.

It was during this season in the life of this family that a challenge would present itself to them. Naomi strongly suggested to her two daughters-in-law to move on with their lives. She added that they should find husbands and remarry and carry on with their lives.

Here's where many of us, who walk by faith, find ourselves. Should I stay or should I go?

Decisions, Decisions, Decisions!

"So she kissed them, and they lifted up their voices and wept. And they said to her, 'Surely we will return with you to your people.'"

After Naomi makes the suggestion for them to go back to their mother's houses, these two ladies had to make a choice. Let us dive a little deeper and see their hearts.

They both were kissed by their mother-in-law— they both lifted up their voices and wept; they both said, **"Surely we will return with you to your people."**

But did they? Or who did?

Listen to Naomi's reply after they said they would come back to Judah with her: **"But Naomi said, 'Turn back, my daughters; why will you go with me? Are there still sons in my womb, that they may be your husbands? Turn back, my daughters, go—for I am too old to have a husband...'"**

Logically speaking, Naomi was right! What in God's name were they going to do if they came back home with her? It made no sense to come back home with her now did it?

She had no other children who were older, and if she was to have children that very day, Ruth and Orpah would probably be way too old to marry them by the time they grew up!

No Power to Sustain God's Given Vision!

"Then they lifted up their voices and wept again..." Apparently, Naomi's words were so strong and convincing that both of their hearts were deeply challenged.

They now had to make a decision like one they had never made before. Their backs were against the wall! It was now or never! Oh, my dear God, have you ever been at this place in your own walk with God?

Can you imagine how these words must have sounded and resounded in their ears going so deep to the point of reaching their human spirit? The echo of these (life-changing, life-altering, and future-forming) words replaying in their heads over and over again in a period of 10 seconds?

When God Doesn't Make Sense!

"...and Orpah kissed her mother-in-law, but Ruth clung to her."

The next few minutes would be very telling on both of these two daughters-in-law. The Scripture says that **"Orpha kissed her mother-in-law** [goodbye]**."**

Orpah saw the logic to all this and parted ways. Her common-sense did not allow her to see any possibility or an opportunity for that matter.

In the case of Ruth, the Scripture says that she clung to Naomi. What does the word clung mean? The word clung means to hold on firmly or tenaciously with the hand.

Ruth was not going to have no for an answer. She was going to hold on until something greater would appear. Her decision didn't make any sense! Oftentimes God doesn't make a lot of sense!

I believe that people who see in the spirit, always see God's intent. They see possibilities, they see opportunities, etc.

As I close this meditation, I want to challenge you to a

walk with God that leads to purpose. A walk that brings you to a higher place in God!

So, will you kiss your future goodbye? Or will you cling to it?

Neh'enah.

51

Emptied-Out! Part 1

"Now the two of them went until they came to Bethlehem. And it happened, when they had come to Bethlehem, that all the city was excited because of them; and the women said, 'Is this Naomi?' But she said to them, 'Do not call me Naomi; call me Mara, for the Almighty has dealt very bitterly with me. I went out full, and the Lord has brought me home again empty. Why do you call me Naomi, since the Lord has testified against me, and the Almighty has afflicted me?'" (Ruth 1:19-21)

This afternoon, after a hard day of work outdoors, mowing the lawn, trimming the trees and building stuff, I realized I've had something on my mind that I had previously meditated on.

I'm speaking of the Book of Ruth. What a tremendous

revelation God has been unfolding to me in the last few days – all found in the book of Ruth chapter 1.

If you are familiar with the story of Ruth, it basically starts with Elimelech and his wife Naomi and their children, leaving from Bethlehem, Judah to the country of Moab.

Apparently, a famine had hit Judah, and they left with the hopes of finding something better in Moab. Aside from this one motive, I cannot assume more, yet I know that sometimes when people leave geographical places, it is usually for a good reason – but not always!

Now, sometimes we tend to leave too early, sometimes too late and sometimes we don't leave when we should.

In regard to moving, our motives also play a big role. Sometimes we think we will get more of what we desire, be it money, influence, position, better opportunities, etc.

While we ponder our move, sometimes we feel it's the Holy Spirit leading us, sometimes it's an alluring opportunity, and sometimes it's plain convenience and/or preference.

I believe I have lived long enough and have moved around enough to know that our motives for moving vary in degree.

If things go well, we say it was God! If things go bad, we say it was our flesh, or someone seduced us to pursue something intriguing.

Be it what it may, all moves carry their own consequences and blessings.

When the Bottom Falls Off!

After being in Moab for some time, Elimelech (Naomi's husband) died. After him their two sons (Mahlon and Chilion) died. Not only did all those three men die, but they were all married.

A Turn of Events!

It was then that this successful story took a turn for the worse, or was it for the worse?

I think that too often we are blinded by our natural state of affairs and can lose sight of Almighty God and His sovereignty— and how it all plays a part in our daily lives!

Naomi becomes a widow, her two daughters-in-law become widows, and everything that looked promising went to nothing!

Have you been there my friend? Has God ever taken you to the backside of the desert? It is definitely not a happy or joyful moment!

In spite of all that took place, one needs to always have the sense that something greater is about to take place.

It is almost as if we are checkers on a checkerboard, and God is moving the checkers where they need to be, so He will receive greater glory! Neh'enah.

52

Emptied-Out! Part 2

Today, I want to continue building on this message of being Emptied-Out.

Most people don't realize how God moves in their lives, but He does. The way He aligns things to be, how He sets up things for greater fruition, all of it. He is an amazing God!

The Challenge to Stay Behind

In regard to the widows Naomi, Ruth, and Orpah:

I don't know how long this family was in duress; I don't know how painful their ordeal was, but I can imagine the emotional pain and heartache.

I have experienced the loss of a loved one, and it is not a fun place to be.

Naomi gets a report that things have been changing back home in Bethlehem and that the Lord had visited His people once again. Taking into account this fact, she decides to go back home to Bethlehem, Judah and start a new life once again.

The only difference now, was that she had two daughters-in-law that had been living with her, and now she had to decide to leave them behind.

This was also not an easy thing, but made her request known to them and recommended that they stay back in Moab and start new lives themselves.

Orpah stayed behind in Moab, but Ruth followed Naomi back to Judah.

"Is this Naomi?"

"Now the two of them went until they came to Bethlehem. And it happened, when they had come to Bethlehem, that all the city was excited because of them; and the women said, 'Is this Naomi?'"

I want you to pay special attention to the events that followed here.

I am not sure how much time had elapsed since Elimelech and Naomi had left Bethlehem, Judah, but apparently everyone (and I'm assuming neighbors and friends, etc.) recognized her when she got back to Bethlehem.

The Scripture says, **"...that all the city was excited because of them..."**

Can you imagine the exuberance?

All the city wanted to hear how the trip went. They all wanted to know how their kids had grown up and whether they got married and perhaps how many children they had or even ask Naomi, "Are you a grandmother now?"

Can you picture this? How do you explain your situation (in the most sensitive way) without making them feel bad for asking without knowing the facts, especially your family, friends, and acquaintances?

By reading the text, we can conclude that Naomi did not have an issue expressing or manifesting her brokenness and bitter soul!

Here is what she said, **"Do not call me Naomi; call me Mara, for the Almighty has dealt very bitterly with me."**

Can you hear the hush that came over the people…it must have been deafening!

The Name Naomi Means

I want to bring forth something very deep here:

First, the name Naomi in the Hebrew language means,

"pleasantness." There was a time when Naomi walked in the pleasantness of spirit. She was agreeable, delightful, and blessed.

The circumstances that came upon her did a number on her. She was broken by them! She could hardly remember that at one time she used to be pleasant but now all this was gone!

She had succumbed to the breaking by the trial she had gone through. She was in such deep pain and struggle that she didn't see anything pleasant in her life.

The second thing that she mentions is this, **"...call me Mara, for the Almighty has dealt very bitterly with me."**

The word Mara means "bitter." There is no doubt that she was under intense grief following the death of her husband and children. Wouldn't anyone?

Started Full and Ended Up Empty!

"I went out full, and the Lord has brought me home again empty."

As I meditated upon this one particular verse, I discovered such a revealing truth to most of our ventures in life.

I don't think anyone sets themselves up for failure on purpose! I don't think people plan to go through the ringer just because they have nothing better to do. I don't think people enter a state of grief just because they are bored with reality tv!

When we set our sail to reach great heights or great opportunities, we set our hearts on having great success.

Our emotions are engaged; our minds are in tune; our spirits are soaring with faith, and our vision is clear!

Yet in all our planning and strategy, there is an emptying that accompanies it. The emptying process is not a process for the weak, but for those who have seen a glimpse of the future.

Naomi moved with her husband believing for bigger and better things! They had their hearts set on building themselves a great future!

Yes, all they ever wanted was to overcome the economical deficit back home and find a great breakthrough in Moab!

None of it happened as planned. It wasn't supposed to be this way!

Naomi said, **"I went out full, and the Lord has brought me home again empty."**

When it comes to our walk with Christ, He wants to be everything to us. He doesn't need our help to make anything happen; He only wants our cooperation! He wants to be your Source and mine! He wants to be the One who fills our cup on a daily basis.

Anything other than Jesus that fills you, is an illusion. If you sow to the flesh, (as the Scripture says) we will reap corruption!

Naomi teaches us that one can leave anywhere, to any place at any time, with whatever motive of your choosing, but it will be the Lord that will direct your steps and bring you to His desired end!

Don't Beat Yourself Down!

As I close these thoughts, I want you to realize something about this passage here in Ruth 1.

I saw something that brought me much comfort: **"Do not call me Naomi; call me Mara."**

Please notice that in her bitterness and in her pain, Naomi said, **"Do not call me Naomi; call me Mara."**

When we are in pain, we tend to look down on ourselves. We tend to evaluate ourselves in the worst of ways. This is almost a natural thing we do when the bottom falls off!

The good thing here is this: Naomi was calling herself Mara! It was not God calling her Mara! Bless the Lord forevermore!

In God's eyes, Naomi was still that woman God made to be pleasant!

If we continue to trust God, He will take us through any situation; yes, God is able to make us stand and restore the joy and peace in the Holy Spirit back to us!

If he named us pleasant, it's because that is the nature He intends for us to live by!

"Now to Him who is able to keep you from stumbling, and to make you stand in the presence of His glory blameless with great joy, to the only God our Savior, through Jesus Christ our Lord, beglory, majesty, dominion and authority, before all time and now and forever." Amen. (Jude 24) Neh'enah.

Ministry Information

For more information regarding the ministry of Masterbuilder Ministries, Inc., preaching engagements, leadership conferences, Vessels Seminars (Leadership Training Seminars,) Masterbuilder School of Ministry or bookstore, please, feel free to email David Mayorga at:

david_mayorga@sbcglobal.net
mayorga1126@gmail.com

Also, feel free to check out our minstry websites:
www.masterbuildertx.com
www.dmayorga.com
www.shabarpublications.com

You can locate our ministry base at this address:

Masterbuilder Ministries, Inc.
3833 N. Taylor Rd.
Palmhurst, Texas 78573

Ministry Resources
Other Books by David Mayorga

THE FEW
A Call to the Road Less Traveled-The Call to Intimacy with God

ISBN - 9780999171004

LOS POCOS
Un Llamado al Camino Menos Transitado - El Llamado a la Intimidad Con Dios.
(*Spanish Version of The Few.*)
ISBN - 9780999171028

All Books Available at
www.shabarpublications.com

The Heart of David Journal

Volume 4

The Heart of David Journal

The Heart of David Journal

The Heart of David Journal

www.ingramcontent.com/pod-product-compliance
Lightning Source LLC
Chambersburg PA
CBHW021821090426
42811CB00028B/1936
9781733317412